Jude's Kitchen

Judie Steeves

Jude's Kitchen

OKANAGAN INSTITUTE

LIBRARY AND ARCHIVES CANADA
CATALOGUING IN PUBLICATION
Jude's Kitchen
Judie Steeves
ISBN 978-0-9810271-9-7
A catalogue record for this publication is available
from the National Library of Canada.

Photographs by Judie Steeves
Publisher and designer: Robert MacDonald
Printed in Canada by Aspire Media Works, Kelowna BC.

Creative
Engagement

Produced and published by the Okanagan Institute
1473 Ethel Street, Kelowna BC V1Y 2X9 Canada
www.okanaganinstitute.com

10 9 8 7 6 5 4 3 2 1

Table of Contents

Table of Photographs

Photos, in order of their appearance in the book – page numbers of recipes before, and photos after:

Dedication

This book is the culmination of decades of time spent in the kitchen, joyously tasting and trying new flavours out on family and friends, so I must dedicate it to all of them.

My husband Dennis has been incredibly patient over the years, waiting for a photo to be taken of his dinner while it cooled off, before he got to eat; and yet still willing to taste-test another creation from Jude's Kitchen. Not only that, but he does the dishes too! Thanks dear.

And, for my daughters Gillian and Emily, who are always foremost in my thoughts when I write about food, because my goal is to grow healthy families and children, eager to try new foods and determined to focus on what's local and in season.

And, thanks to my dear friend, home economist and extraordinary cook, Jan Waldon, who slogged through the entire manuscript and cleaned it up.

Additionally, many thanks to fellow newspaper reporter and author John Schreiner, an authority on B.C. and Canadian wines, for adding his margin notes on which wines would pair best with many of my recipes.

You'll find his books on the wineries of this province an invaluable adjunct to Jude's Kitchen and great fun on a tour of the province, or just for reference.

His current titles include: The Wineries of British Columbia, third edition (Whitecap Books, 2009), John Schreiner's Okanagan Wine Tour Guide, third edition (Whitecap Books, 2010), and John Schreiner's B.C. Coastal Wine Tour Guide (Whitecap Books, 2011).

Finally, to Anita Stewart, founder of Cuisine Canada, a national alliance of people determined to encourage the use and recognition of fine Canadian food and wine, who inspired me to consider the word 'locavore' and who urged me to join Cuisine Canada.

Both she and the world-class chefs now serving the foodies of the Okanagan—while bringing the world here to drink and dine—have been inspirational in my thinking and writing about food.

Thank-you so much.

Foreword

This is a book about B.C. food.

It's organized seasonally, beginning with the first sprouts of spring that pop up in various areas of the province and carrying through to the dead of winter when the freshest food is that which was preserved properly earlier in the year, either by freezing, canning, drying, fermenting or keeping at the perfect temperature and atmospheric conditions – or that grown in greenhouses or in the temperate climate of the coast.

It features wild Pacific salmon and snapper, shrimp and prawns; Fraser Valley potatoes, pork and poultry, berries and dairy products, mushrooms and vegetables; beef and lamb from the Cariboo; grains from the Peace River region; tree fruits, grapes and wine from the orchards and vineyards of the Okanagan; and the fruit, vegetables and dairy products of the Kootenays.

This province boasts the most diverse agriculture of any part of Canada, and that's something to celebrate.

That diversity provides the makings of a very exciting food and wine culture and those fresh and inspirational raw materials have drawn some of the world's top chefs to B.C.

Anyone cooking in B.C. has the best opportunity in this country to jump on the Eat Local bandwagon, yet still have a palette of flavourful food available to them.

Eating what's produced as near as possible to your kitchen not only provides your family with the tastiest and most nutritious meals, but also means you are improving the economic conditions in your own community, to your benefit, while supporting local farmers and small business people.

On a broader scale, it also supports the health of the planet by reducing our carbon footprint. Transporting products half-way around the world is costly in many different ways.

What's needed to make it work is a change in attitude. Who needs to eat fresh tomatoes in mid-winter? The ones plucked off the vine, still warm from the sun in mid-summer, are worth waiting half a year for. It's all about your outlook. In winter, enjoy frozen or canned tomatoes in different dishes. Instead of a salad, think sauce.

Even more importantly, consider the future, and what it could be like if we don't support local farmers now. Imagine the loss of verdant green fields, orchards and vineyards – and the loss of fresh flavours – if we lose those farms to concrete and asphalt.

In the process we will also lose control of what's going into our food if we have to import it all from other countries.

Within these pages, I hope you'll find a treasure trove of recipes that excite your spirit and soothe the soul, while encouraging you to be inspired by what's in season locally.

As you leaf through this book, jot down the page numbers of recipes that look intriguing and tuck that paper into the front of the book to refer to when you're wondering what to cook next.

I hope you come up with a nice, long list.

Introduction

Everyone cooks differently, and I wouldn't dream of trying to stifle that creativity; the individuality that sets each person's cooking style apart from everyone else—but it's only fair that I offer information about how I cook, since that's the basis for these recipes.

You'll need this information to understand how I prepare the recipes you'll find in this book. Then, you can make whatever changes you wish to them. Think outside the box.

In the introduction to some recipes, I suggest some possible substitutions, but before making any recipe, you should always read it all the way through, in case there are some other suggestions in the instructions you want to use.

Butter/margarine

When I cook, I frequently make substitutions. For instance, sometimes I want the flavour of butter in a sauce or other dish, so I might use a combination of olive oil and butter because that allows me to cook at a slightly higher temperature without browning the butter.

I never cook with margarine, but in some instances, you can substitute margarine when a recipe calls for butter. You may get quite a different result if you substitute soft margarine though, because it contains more water.

Dairy products

I tend to use lower fat options such as part-skim milk; fat-free yogurt; lower-fat cheeses and even low-fat sour cream. However, sometimes only whipping cream will do. In other instances, the low-fat options are just as flavourful and better for most of us.

Produce

For the best flavour and nutrition, the freshest ingredients are the best. I'm not a big fan of canned vegetables, except tomatoes; chickpeas or garbanzo beans; and kidney beans.

The same applies to frozen vegetables, except spinach, which can frequently be substituted for fresh when it is to be cooked. I've found that a pound of fresh spinach is about the equivalent of a half-package of frozen, or five ounces, and about a cup of cooked spinach. I also use frozen peas occasionally.

I'm not fanatical about it, but I do like organic produce, in part because those farmers have to pay more attention to their crops in order to keep ahead of pests and disease, so they're very carefully grown. In grapes and wine, there's little advantage.

I use a lot of garlic and onions. When slicing onions, if you cut them in half first, they stay steady on your chopping board for the rest of your cutting.

Whole grain/processed

Whenever possible I use whole grains, but sometimes my breads and muffins are not as light as they would otherwise be. They make up for it in flavour and food value.

Instead of sifting flour, I use a whisk to mix those ingredients and keep them light.

Herbs

Wherever possible, I use fresh herbs. However, in the dead of winter in B.C., that's not always possible. Some herbs do not dry well, including parsley and basil, so you're generally better off to substitute something else, like basil paste or oil; or another herb if you can't get fresh. Others dry beautifully, including rosemary, thyme and sage. Use a third to half the amount of dried herb to get a similar flavour to fresh, if substituting. Taste as you go.

Exotic ingredients

In stir-fry recipes, I've found that ground bean sauce, brown bean sauce and bean sauce are interchangeable. All are generally available at Asian specialty stores or sections in grocery stores.

Most of the ingredients called for in my recipes are readily available, but you may have to search out a few special items for some recipes.

When my recipes call for these ingredients, I've used:

- flour: unbleached white
- egg: large egg
- oil: grapeseed for high heat
- oil: extra virgin olive otherwise
- sugar: white
- salt: sea salt
- yeast: fast acting

With today's instant global communications and jet transport, our repertoire of favourite foods has grown immensely, crossing cultural borders and fusing foods from many countries in a single dish.

It's made cooking and eating much more exciting, with new experiences around every corner.

Enjoy them all.

John Schreiner's tasting notes

Good food is greatly enhanced by fine wine and we are very lucky in this province to have access to a wide variety of very good, locally-produced wines.

So, it was with much excitement that I learned John Schreiner could make time to put together tasting notes for many of the recipes you'll find within these pages. You'll find them in the margins of the text, along with comments on pairing wine and different food flavours.

His expertise is an invaluable addition for those who enjoy pairing food and wine.

John is Canada's most prolific author of wine books, and is the recipient of the Founders' Award, presented by the Okanagan Wine Festivals Society, recognizing his contribution to the wine industry; as well as the Spirited Industry Professional Award, presented by the Vancouver Playhouse International Wine Festival.

He also is a popular wine judge, and he writes a blog: johnschreiner.blogspot.com

Spring

1. Sprouts & Greens

THE SPROUTS OF SPRING

The sprouting of B.C. asparagus in spring is the beginning of the arrival of all manner of delicately-flavoured local baby vegetables such as miniature bok choy, little peapods, fresh, slim green onions and crisp young greens.

Almost all of them are delicious quickly stir-fried with a bit of spicy sauce and a few slivers of lean meat such as B.C. boneless chicken, pork, beef or seafood. The rest are best raw, tossed in a salad with a light splash of dressing and a few toasted nuts, a little fish, meat or cheese on the side.

This is a great way to cook if you're interested in lean, nutritious, flavourful meals. There's just a little meat, so it's an economical way to feed a family as well.

The variety in a stir-fry makes the dish not only attractive and appetizing-looking, but also packed with the vitamins and minerals essential to healthy living.

Another advantage of stir-fries is the possible variations from every recipe. No pork in the freezer? Dig out a chicken breast or thigh. Out of prawns? Substitute scallops, or even beef, if that's what you have available. No asparagus? Try it with bok choy instead. Sugar peas aren't ready yet? Substitute stalks of celery or bok choy, spinach leaves, mustard greens, or collards. And then, there are always fresh bean sprouts, sweet peppers and mushrooms. All fresh, in season, from the fields, farms and greenhouses of B.C.'s farmlands – or your own garden.

Once you start stir-frying simple ingredients in the wok, you'll find yourself just using what's in the fridge or freezer to make delicious, simple, nutritious, reasonably-priced meals for one, two or the whole family.

It's all made in one pot too, so cleaning up after dinner is easy. (Well, actually, there's a second one if you cook rice or chinese noodles to have with it as well.)

Once you begin, remember you can substitute. Just use your imagination and let those creative juices flow.

In my kitchen, a little wine usually flows as well, so it's incredibly lucky that B.C. also produces some of the best wines in the world. If you doubt that, or if you'd like to try a few more of them, taste test some of the latest releases at the Spring Okanagan Wine Festival, held every April and May throughout the Okanagan Valley. It's not as hectic as the popular fall wine festival, and winemakers have a little more time available to share with visitors because they're not trying to harvest the current vintage of grapes at the same time.

For details of the many events, go to www.thewinefestivals.com

Sugar Peas & Pork

Sweet flavors like delicate sugar peas or snow peas are delicious with pork. If it's a little early for peas from your own garden, there may be some in stores. Baby bok choy, cut in half, would be delicious in this as well.

WINE FOR SUGAR PEAS & PORK: *Ehrenfelser, a tangy wine with tropical fruit flavours, would be my choice. Look for CedarCreek or Summerhill or Gray Monk.*

1/2 lb. (225 g) pork strips
1 tbsp. (15 ml) fresh ginger
1/2 lb. (225 g) sugar or snow peas
1 large onion
10 mushrooms
1/2 red pepper
1 tbsp. (15 ml) soy sauce
1 tbsp. (15 ml) hoisin sauce
1/2 tsp. (2 ml) Szechuan sauce
1 tbsp. (15 ml) cornstarch
1/2 c. (125 ml) water
green onions for garnish

- Slice pork tenderloin or other lean meat a quarter-inch thick, then into quarter to half-inch wide strips. Mince ginger root.
- Prepare vegetables, but leave separated so they can be added to the wok at different times. Cut onion into large slivers; string sugar peas; cut mushrooms into quarters; and cut red pepper into strips or small dice.
- Combine cornstarch with a spoonful of cold water in a small bowl, ready to use to thicken the sauce just before serving.
- Heat a drizzle of cooking oil in a wok or a large, deep frypan, then add ginger root. Stir fry about half a minute, then add onion chunks, separating them as you stir and turn them about for a minute or so.
- Add mushrooms and stir-fry for a couple of minutes.
- Sprinkle with a drizzle of soy sauce and a quarter-cup or so of water, add red pepper, then cover to steam them for a couple of minutes.
- Turn out onto the serving platter.
- Re-heat wok, adding the another drizzle of oil.
- Add sliced pork, stirring constantly for a minute or so, until it has lost its pinkness.
- Return vegetable mixture to the wok, stir together, then push it up the sides. Bring the liquid in the middle to a bubble, add hoisin sauce and spicy Szechuan sauce, then cornstarch and water mixture and stir until it thickens and bubbles again. Add more water as needed and combine everything quickly until it's all covered with a translucent glaze, and the sauce suits you. Don't overcook.
- Vegetables should still be vibrantly-colored, not dull and limp.
- Sprinkle platter of food with chopped green onion for garnish.
- Serves three or four; more if part of a Chinese meal.

Prawns with Asparagus

This is a great dish to celebrate the coming of spring, and the sprouting of fresh asparagus. Crunchy chunks of that delectable sprout are excellent stir-fried. Thaw local spot prawns, if fresh aren't available. Dried, fermented black beans are available in Oriental specialty stores, but you could leave them out if they're just not available.

1/2 lb. (227 g) prawns
1 onion
10 or so asparagus stalks
2 celery stalks
6 mushrooms
1 red pepper
1 tbsp. (15 ml) minced fresh ginger
1 tbsp. (15 ml) dried fermented black beans
1 tbsp. (15 ml) light soy sauce
1/2 c. (125 ml) water
1 tbsp. (15 ml) cornstarch
1 tbsp. (15 ml) cold water

- Shell prawns. Trim, rinse and chop asparagus into one-inch pieces. Chop onion and slice celery. Dice red pepper.
- Heat a drizzle of oil in a wok or deep frypan over medium-high heat. Add most of the minced ginger and onion and stir-fry for a few minutes.
- Add asparagus, celery and mushrooms and continue to stir-fry for another couple of minutes. Add red pepper, light soy sauce, and water and put the lid on for just a few minutes to steam the vegetables.
- Remove from the wok to a serving platter.
- Add a drizzle of oil to the wok and add the remaining ginger, prawns and black beans. Cook just until the prawns turn pink and opaque, turning to cook both sides. Add the liquid from the vegetables, bring it to bubbling and add cornstarch and water mixture, stirring until it thickens and turns translucent. Add more water and stir in, if needed.
- Return vegetables and stir gently until they are coated with sauce.
- Serve with steamed Chinese noodles or rice.
- Serves 2 to 3.

See photograph on page **17**

WINE FOR PRAWNS WITH ASPARAGUS: *I recommend a Riesling (Tantalus, Intrigue, Quails' Gate, Orofino) or a Chenin Blanc (Quails' Gate, Inniskillin Okanagan or Road 13).*

Asparagus & Sesame Salad

Steam a half- pound to a pound (220 g to 454 g) of asparagus tips for six minutes or so, or until just tender. Drain well and arrange in a serving dish.

DRESSING:
1/2 c. (125 ml) nuts
1 tbsp. (15 ml) sesame oil
1/4 c. (60 ml) cider vinegar
1/4 c. (60 ml) soy sauce
1/3 c. (75 ml) sugar
freshly-ground black pepper
roasted sesame seeds

- Chop walnuts, pecans, or other nuts finely. Mix together with remaining ingredients and pour over asparagus. Add a sprinkle of freshly-ground black pepper.
- Serve immediately or marinate for two or three hours before serving slightly chilled, garnished with roasted sesame seeds.
- Do not marinate overnight.

WINE FOR ASPARAGUS & SESAME SALAD: *Given the savoury flavours, this would pair well with a Riesling Icewine.*

WINE FOR SHRIMP & FRUIT BUNDLES: *I recommend a blended white like Stoneboat's Chorus or JoieFarm's A Noble Blend, where the sweet core of fruit flavours picks up the tropical fruits in the dish.*

Shrimp & Fruit Bundles

We don't grow papayas in B.C., but they are delicious in this. You could substitute mango. B.C. nectarines or peaches are also a nice match with the shrimp in this pretty and a refreshing bite to tease the appetite.

The Cucumber Dill Dip can also be served with a platter of colourful, fresh, raw vegetables; or with crisp, dried pita chips.

soft lettuce leaves, as wrappers
1/2 papaya, peeled and diced
1/4 lb. (112 g) prawns or shrimp
toasted sesame seeds, to garnish

CUCUMBER DILL DIP:
1/4 c. (60 ml) minced cucumber
1/4 c. (60 ml) plain yogurt
1 tbsp. (15 ml) fresh parsley
1 tbsp. (15 ml) fresh chives
1 tbsp. (15 ml) fresh dill, minced
1/2 tsp. (2 ml) honey
1/2 tsp. (2 ml) sea salt
1/8 tsp. (.5 ml) fresh ground black pepper

- Rinse and dry small, soft lettuce leaves such as those from butter lettuce, as wraps.
- Put a dab of dip, a prawn or a couple of shrimp on each leaf. Top with a cube of fruit and wrap it up.
- You could substitute avocado for the fruit, but it's not as colourful.

See photograph on page **17**

IN SPRINGS PADDY'S DAY

Usually we can celebrate both St. Patrick's Day and spring in the same week. It's a double excuse to wear my favourite colour: green.

There is much controversy and few facts surrounding one of Ireland's patron saints, St. Patrick, but it would seem he was a Christian missionary, for whom this annual feast day, St. Patrick's Day, was named. It's a national holiday in Ireland.

In the Americas, St. Paddy's Day has become a grand excuse to discover the slightest of Irish blood in one's ancestry and celebrate with a pint of green beer and some great pub food.

Whether you have Irish stew, a plate of shepherd's pie or some of the many variations on the staple of Irish life, the potato, doesn't really matter.

Even more important is the Spring Equinox, when day and night are of equal length, and the days begin to get longer than the hours of darkness. Hurrah!

That means it's the beginning of spring, and the official end of another long, dark winter.

So, dust off the barbecue and haul out some meat from the freezer; check the ground where your chives were, so you can capture those first little green shoots to snip into some scrambled eggs on the weekend. Yum.

Two excuses to celebrate. I can do that!

TOP:
Prawns & Asparagus

Recipe on page 14

BOTTOM:
Shrimp & Fruit Bundles

Recipe on page 15

TOP:
Wendy's Shepherd's Pie

Recipe on

page **22**

BOTTOM:
Egg & Potato Flip

Recipe on

page **23**

TOP:
**Steak &
Sunflower
Seed Salad**

Recipe on
page **26**

BOTTOM:
**Soy &
Sesame
Steak**

Recipe on
page **27**

TOP:
Curry Peanut Sauce
Recipe on page **29**

BOTTOM:
Skewers of Barbequed Prawns
Recipe on page **32**

Microwave Rhubarb Crisp

Rhubarb is another spring sprout that is delicious as well as nutritious, although you don't have to tell anyone that. Not everyone is a fan of rhubarb, which is a shame, because it's very good for you.

The recipe can be adapted fairly simply to make a microwave dessert using apples, blueberries or other fruit.

TOPPING:
1 c. (250 ml) brown sugar
1/2 c. (125 ml) flour
1/2 c. (125 ml) oats
1/2 tsp. (2 ml) nutmeg
1/4 c. (60 ml) butter

■ Combine dry ingredients, then cut in butter or margarine until the mixture looks like coarse crumbs.

FRUIT:
6 c. (1.5 l) rhubarb, diced
1/4 c. (60 ml) apple juice

■ Butter an eight-inch casserole dish, add the fruit and sprinkle a bit of liquid over it. You can use water, wine or apple juice.
■ Crumble topping mixture over fruit, then microwave, uncovered, on high for 15 minutes, or until fruit is tender when pierced with a fork.
Serve warm with whipping cream or ice cream, if desired.
Serves 5 or 6.

Pat's Rhubarb Oat Squares

This great-tasting dessert made with rhubarb, is similar to the matrimonial squares made with dates.

3 c. (750 ml) oats
2 c. (500 ml) brown sugar
3 c. (750 ml) flour
2 tsp. (10 ml) baking powder
1 tsp. (5 ml) baking soda
1/2 tsp. (2 ml) salt
2 c. (500 ml) butter

FILLING:
6 c. (1.5 ml) cut-up rhubarb
3 c. (750 ml) brown sugar
2 tsp. (10 ml) vanilla
1/4 c. (60 ml) cornstarch
a little cold water

■ Pre-heat oven to 350 F.
■ Combine dry ingredients and cut in butter with a pastry cutter until it's like bread crumbs. Press about two-thirds of the mixture into a large, greased pan, 13x9 inches.
■ Combine all filling ingredients in a pot and cook over medium heat until thickened, using as little water as possible to prevent it from sticking to the pot.
■ Cover the base with the rhubarb filling and top with remaining oat mixture, patting it gently into place.
■ Bake for about 20 to 30 minutes and cool before cutting into squares.

WINE FOR MICROWAVE RHUBARB CRISP: *With this, I would serve a late harvest dessert wine, which is neither as intense as Icewine nor as expensive. Some examples: Quails' Gate's Botrytized Optima and Thornhaven's Nectar del Sol.*

WINE FOR PAT'S RHUBARB OAT SQUARES: *I'd like a Gehringer Brothers Ehrenfelser Icewine or a Sonoran Estate Oraniensteiner Icewine.*

Wendy's Shepherd's Pie

Simple, but comforting and delicious, this traditional favourite from the British Isles is perfect to serve for St. Patrick's Day dinner. You could update or vary this basic recipe by adding a cup of cheddar cheese to the potato topping; by adding an envelope of taco seasoning to the meat mixture; or spice it up a bit with Worcestershire sauce and hot sauce.

2 minced garlic cloves
1 large onion, diced
1/2 lb. (227 g) mushrooms
3 carrots, diced
1 celery stalk, diced
drizzle of oil
2 lb. (1 kg) lean ground beef
1 tbsp. (15 ml) flour
3/4 c. (175 ml) beef stock
salt and pepper, to taste
garlic mashed potatoes

- Pre-heat oven to 350 Γ.
- Soften the vegetables by sauteing in a frypan over medium heat in a drizzle of oil.
- Remove them from the pan and brown the ground beef in it, sprinkling with the flour and cooking for a couple of minutes longer.
- Add the beef stock, a little at a time, stirring it in until it thickens.
- Return the vegetables to the pan and stir it all together. You could add a cup of peas at this point.
- Put into a deep pie pan or casserole and top with the garlic mashed potatoes.
- Freeze until another day, or put into the oven for about an hour.
- Serves 4 to 6.

See photograph on page **18**

WINE FOR WENDY'S SHEPHERD'S PIE: *This calls for a robust red like Van Westen's Voluptuous, Fairview Cellars Madcap Red or Desert Hills Mirage.*

Egg & Potato Flip

This is one of my favourite weekend brunch dishes, but it could also be served for lunch, or with a steak or chop for dinner.

2 potatoes
1 onion
2 tbsp. (30 ml) Swiss cheese
1 tbsp. (15 ml) pepperoni, ham or bacon
salt and pepper to taste
2 eggs
1 tbsp. (15 ml) butter

- Scrub potatoes, but do not peel, and grate into a medium-sized bowl.
- Add finely chopped onion, grated Swiss cheese, minced meat, and salt and pepper to taste.
- Beat eggs and add, combining everything well.
- Melt butter over medium-high heat, in a frypan large enough to hold it all. I sometimes use an electric pan, but a large cast iron pan or a non-stick frypan works well. So does a griddle.
- You could make individual "pan-cakes" by pressing spoonfuls onto the hot pan, or cook it all in one mass and then use a spatula to cut it into wedges to turn.
- Cook until the underside is nicely browned, then flip.
- Cook for 20 minutes or so, until the potatoes are cooked, turning as necessary.
- Serves 2-4.

See photograph on page **18**

Green Rice

Greens such as spinach and collards are delicious and nutritious cooked with rice for a quick mix of vegetables and a starch. Toss a little leftover chicken or beef on top for a fast meal after work.

1 onion
3 c. (750 ml) fresh greens
2 tsp. (10 ml) butter
1 c. (250 ml) white rice
2 c. (500 ml) chicken stock
salt and pepper, to taste

- Mince onion. Rinse and chop greens such as spinach, Swiss chard or collards (they're fabulous in this, if you can find them).
- Melt butter in a large pot over medium heat and soften the onion in it, stirring. Add the greens and stir until they've wilted, then add the rice and chicken stock or water, salt and freshly-ground black pepper, to your taste.
- Bring to a bubble, then mix well and turn down to simmering, covered with a tight-fitting lid.
- Cook without peeking for about 20 minutes or until the rice is cooked through and the liquid absorbed.
- Serves 2 or 3.

WINE FOR EGG & POTATO FLIP:
Serve this at brunch or lunch with a crisp sparkling wine like See Ya Later Ranch Brut or Salt Spring Vineyards Karma

WINE FOR GREEN RICE:
This calls for an unoaked Chardonnay (JoieFarm, Gray Monk) or a light Riesling (Kettle Valley, Gehringer Brothers)

Green-stuffed Spicy Spuds

There are infinite variations on the old stuffed, baked potatoes, but this is one that's particularly good, with the bit of a kick from jalapenos. Add as little or as much as you like, and feel free to add a little chili pepper to spice them up a little further. These could serve as an entire meal.

4 large russet potatoes
3 green onions
1/4 red pepper
1 minced jalapeno, or more
1/4 c. (125 ml) plain yogurt
1/2 c. (125 ml) cheese
salt and freshly-grated black pepper
4 c. (1 l) spinach leaves

- Preheat oven to 350 Γ.
- Bake scrubbed, pricked whole potatoes in the oven for about 30 minutes, or until soft enough to scoop out the insides.
- Mince green onions, red pepper and jalapeno pepper and set aside. Grate cheese such as cheddar or Swiss. Chop the spinach and barely wilt it in the microwave or on the stove.
- Slice off the top of the spud and carefully scoop out the flesh inside the skin, leaving a quarter-inch or so as your shell.
- Add the remaining ingredients to the bowl with the potato flesh, except for four spoonfuls of grated cheese for the topping and mix together well.
- Carefully spoon the filling back into the potato shells and top with reserved cheese.
- Bake for 20 minutes more or until the cheese melts.
- You can prepare them ahead of time, refrigerate, then pop them into the oven to reheat and melt the cheese, but bake for at least 30 minutes, to ensure they're heated through.
- Serves 4.

WINE FOR GREEN-STUFFED SPICY SPUDS:
This calls for a red – an inexpensive Cabernet Merlot blend.

Irish Stew

This variation on an old favourite has a bit of a twist. I don't know if the Irish would put minced ginger in stew, but we find it adds a slightly spicy, mellow flavour. This re-heats perfectly. We served it over little boiled potatoes the first time, and over brown rice when we re-heated it.

This could also be made in the crockpot or slow cooker by browning the beef and onions as described, then putting them into the crockpot and deglazing the pan with the beer and stock. Pour that over all the ingredients in the slow cooker. Cook for 8 hours on low.

2 lb. (1 kg) stew beef
1/4 c. (60 ml) flour
1/2 tsp. (2 ml) salt
1/2 tsp. (2 ml) pepper
drizzle of oil
2 small onions
1 large garlic clove
1 tbsp. fresh ginger
2 large carrots
2 celery stalks
1 1/2 c. (355 ml) dark beer
1/2 c. (125 ml) beef stock
1 tbsp. (15 ml) fresh rosemary
12 small whole mushrooms

WINE FOR IRISH STEW:
This demands a bold, brambly Cabernet Franc (Fairview Cellars, Herder, Nichol, Tinhorn Creek) or something novel like the Tannat from Moon Curser.

- Coat cubes of lean beef in a mixture of the flour, salt and pepper. You could turn them around in it in a bowl or on wax paper, or in a paper bag.
- Quarter onions and mince garlic and ginger.
- Heat a drizzle of oil in a heavy Dutch oven over medium-high heat and put in the minced fresh ginger and as many beef cubes as you can fit in one layer. Don't stir until the one side has browned, then turn over to brown the other sides. Don't let them burn.
- Add minced garlic and quartered onions and stir in.
- Chop carrots and celery and add.
- Pour beer and beef stock over the browned beef to release all the brown bits from the bottom of the pot. Heat until it bubbles and begins to thicken.
- Mince fresh rosemary and stir in with the whole mushrooms.
- Turn heat to low and let simmer, covered, for a couple of hours or until the beef and vegetables are tender.
- Serves 4 to 6.

2. Spring to the BBQ

COOKING OUTSIDE

When I first wake on an early spring morning, I can hear the birds calling and I realize how quiet they were all winter.

One morning I'll hear the rain, and realize snow is silent when it falls all winter.

I hate doing dishes, so I like to barbecue. It creates fewer of the worst dishes to clean up: roasting pans and stew pots.

So, haul out your barbecue, dust it off and fire it up.

There's nothing quite like the aroma and flavour of smoky, barbecued ribs or chicken, but try asparagus and baby bok choy on the barbecue as well, and you may be as pleased as I was.

We've always loved little red potatoes cooked for a minute or two each in the microwave, then finished up on the barbecue.

As far as the meat goes, your options are almost endless and go far beyond the ordinary steak, chops and ribs, to salmon, snapper, shrimp, lamb, chicken in all its forms, and roasts.

Kebabs are a bit of a nuisance to put together, but once that's done, dinner's ready. You can do separate meat and vegetable skewers, or mix the two on the same stick. I use metal skewers, but if you use wooden ones make sure you soak them first.

With kebabs you can marinate tough cuts of meat first to tenderize them, then spear the chunks along with bits of onion, zucchini, cherry tomatoes, peppers, pineapple, scallops or prawns.

A side of rice, pasta or a spud, and you're all set.

I cook outside all year round, but it's difficult to cook part of the meal outside and part in. Delegate someone else to look after inside stuff, if everything can't be done on the barbecue or its side burner.

There's one more thing I love about barbecuing: the leftovers. Skewer some bits of boneless chicken that's been marinated in a Greek blend of fresh herbs, olive oil and lemon, and you've got the makings for a second meal with the cold chicken popped into a pita half with tzatziki, chopped up peppers and tomato.

Barbecue an extra marinated steak or pieces of chicken and slice up the leftovers the next night to toss into a salad.

How simple is that?

When you're planning meals, let your inspiration be the season. Peruse the garden or the shelves of your local market or farmer's produce stand for ideas.

It's vital we support our own farmers; that we purchase as much of our food as we can close to home.

It's healthier to use products that are as fresh and local as possible, whether that means grown on our own place or purchased locally.

It's also healthier for our communities if our food choices support our neighbours.

And, it's healthier for our environment to expend the least in non-renewable energy to get our food from where it's grown to our tables. The jet fuel required to get peapods from China to B.C. in the off-season is a luxury we can't afford, environmentally – and they don't have the flavour of fresh ones grown here at home anyway.

Soy & Sesame Steak

Chuck blade steaks vary in tenderness, so it's best to marinate them overnight before cooking, to ensure tenderness. A simmering steak tenderizes well in this teriyaki-type marinade. Do extra and you have another quick and nutritious meal later in the week: (see Steak & Sunflower Seed Salad).

1.5 lb. (.75 kg) blade steak
1 tbsp. (15 ml) fresh ginger
1 clove garlic
2 tbsp. (30 ml) soy sauce
1 tbsp. (15 ml) brown sugar
5 drops hot sauce
2 tbsp. (30 ml) sesame seeds
salt and pepper to taste

- Trim fat off meat. Mince ginger and garlic and mix all ingredients together in a glass dish that will hold everything snugly. Poke meat with a fork to allow the marinade to penetrate, and turn meat until all sides are coated. I like to marinate for at least 24 hours in advance, but any period is helpful for tenderizing.
- Remove beef and toss onto preheated barbecue. Grill six to eight minutes a side or until brown and cooked to your taste.
- Remove to a board, and cut to serve, in chunks or slices.
- Serves 4-6.

See photograph on page **19**

WINE FOR SOY & SESAME STEAK: With all the flavours of the marinade at play, I recommend a Syrah (Peller,Nk'Mip, Burrowing Owl, Marichel, Cassini Cellars) or Sperling Vineyards's Old Vines Foch.

WINE FOR GRILLED VEGETABLES: I would serve a fruity rosé with this or a light Gamay Noir. St. Hubertus offers both.

Grilled Vegetables

Thickly slice potatoes, peppers, zucchinis or baby bok choy, or use whole asparagus spears and lay them on the barbecue grill, brushing with different-flavored butters, or spraying them first with a little olive oil. Try adding chives or garlic to your melted butter, or even substitute a barbecue sauce for the butter, for a change. Sprinkle with a little barbecue spice, or freshly-ground sea salt and black pepper.

2-4 russet potatoes
1 tsp. (5 ml) butter, melted
spicy seasonings, to taste

- Cut scrubbed potatoes, length-wise, into 1/4-inch thick slices. Don't bother to peel them, because all the important vitamins are just underneath the skin, and, besides, they're delicious. Halve baby zucchini or bok choy and cut colourful peppers into quarters, lengthwise.
- Lay the slices on the barbecue grill. Brush lightly with melted butter, and sprinkle with spiced pepper or salt, or a non-salt spice.
- Brown on one side, then turn and brown the other, brushing very lightly with butter. If you want criss-cross grill marks, remember to turn them in the other direction on the grill, halfway through cooking.
- They'll cook in five to 15 minutes, depending on the vegetable.
- Don't overcook.

Steak & Sunflower Seed Salad

This is quick to make with meat left over from the barbecued meal a day or two previous. (See Soy & Sesame Steak). You can use a tough cut such as round or blade steak and marinate it overnight before cooking, or use a tender one such as rib eye.

1/2 lb. (225 g) steak
1/2 cucumber
1 mild, sweet onion
1 avocado
4-6 radishes
4 c. (1 l) greens
2 tbsp. (30 ml) sunflower seeds

- Spinach is delicious used alone or combine it with other lettuces or greens. Mustard greens are a tasty addition, or just lettuce could be used.
- Raw mushrooms, thinly-sliced, are another delicious addition to this salad.
- Thinly slice cold, lean steak into two-inch long strips and set aside. (You can vary the amount of meat to your family's taste.)
- Peel and chop cucumber (unless it's an English type which won't need peeling), onion and avocado. Slice radishes.
- Wash, dry and tear greens into a large salad bowl.
- Sprinkle prepared vegetables over the greens, then the thinly-sliced beef steak, and finally the sunflower seeds.
- Serve with a simple dressing such as a balsamic or red wine vinaigrette or a creamy dressing.
- Serves 4.

See photograph on page 19

WINE FOR STEAK AND SUNFLOWER SEED SALAD:
For this, I would serve a robust dry rosé like Distraction from The View Winery or Vailla from Le Vieux Pin.

Meat Sate Marinade

This pairs wonderfully with the Curry-Peanut Sauce. You can use it with beef, chicken or pork.

1 lb. (.5 kg) meat
1 tbsp. (15 ml) honey
2 tsp. (10 ml) soy sauce
2 tsp. (10 ml) cornstarch
2 tsp. (10 ml) minced ginger

- Slice lean meat such as boned chicken breast or thighs; steak; or pork loin into strips just a few inches long, a half-inch wide, and a quarter-inch thick.
- Combine marinade ingredients and stir well, then add meat and mix together thoroughly so meat slices are all coated with marinade. If there doesn't seem to be enough, add a spoonful or so more soy sauce.
- Marinate for just an hour or overnight, before threading onto skewers.
- Grill on a hot barbecue a few minutes on each side, turning to cook all four sides. Don't overcook them until they dry out.
- Greasing the skewers lightly first will reduce the chance of the meat sticking to them. If using wooden skewers be sure to soak them in water first.
- Serves 4-6.

WINE FOR CURRY PEANUT SAUCE: *The best match for the challenge of curry and peanuts is with a dry apple wine, like Adam's Apple from Forbidden Fruit or Elephant Island's Pink Elephant sparkling wine.*

Curry Peanut Sauce

Even the kids will love this and it's great with whatever meat you soak in the Meat Sate Marinade.

1 onion
1 garlic clove
1 tsp. (5 ml) butter
1 tsp. (5 ml) curry powder
3/4 c. (175 ml) crunchy peanut butter
1 tbsp. (15 ml) soy sauce
1 tsp. (5 ml) brown sugar
1 1/2 c. (375 ml) water

- Chop onion finely and mince garlic clove.
- Melt butter in a small pot and add the onions and garlic, sauteing over medium heat until the onion is soft and translucent.
- Add curry powder and stir well, adding crunchy peanut butter, soy sauce and brown sugar and combining well.
- Add water and bring the whole mixture to bubbling. Simmer for 10 minutes or so.
- Serve alongside the skewers as a dip.
- Re-heats well.

See photograph on page **20**

Succulent Yogurt Chicken

Marinating this chicken in yogurt for an hour or overnight is the secret to its tenderness. The flavour's pretty yummy too. It's about as lean a meat as you can get if you use a non-fat yogurt and remove the skin and fat from the chicken parts. It's scrumptious either barbecued or roasted.

Leftovers are terrific cut up into a green salad.

    10 chicken thighs
    1 c. (250 ml) plain yogurt
    3 green onions
    2 tbsp. (30 ml) minced ginger
    2 garlic cloves
    1 tsp. (5 ml) curry powder
    1 tsp. (5 ml) ground cumin
    1 lime
    salt and pepper to taste
    parsley, to garnish

- Skin and trim fat from chicken parts.
- Prepare marinade by putting yogurt into a glass dish with a lid which will hold the chicken snugly.
- Mince green onions, fresh ginger and garlic and add to yogurt along with the minced zest of the lime. Juice the lime into the yogurt mixture and add garam masala or curry powder, cumin and salt and pepper, to taste.
- Combine well and add chicken pieces, turning them about to coat each well. Marinate for an hour or overnight.
- Roast in a 350 F oven on a rack over a tin foil-lined pan for about 30 to 45 minutes, depending on the size of the pieces. Don't overcook.
- You can also barbecue the marinated pieces for about 10 minutes a side, but spray each chicken piece with a little cooking oil before placing on the barbecue to help prevent it from sticking.
- Good cold as well as hot.
- Serves 5-6.

WINE FOR SUCCULENT YOGURT CHICKEN: *This calls for wines with lots of flavour and a little residual sweetness, like Siegerrebe from Larch Hills or Gray Monk or Domaine de Chaberton or Mingle from Noble Ridge.*

Stuffed Barbecued Salmon

There's nothing quite like this dinner with a fresh wild B.C. sockeye salmon. It doesn't have to be boned, but when you stuff it, serving is made much easier and less messy if the bones have been removed ahead of time. It's easier than you think.

5 lb. (2.35 kg) whole Pacific salmon

STUFFING:
3/4 c. (175 ml) celery
3/4 c. (175 ml) onion
1 tbsp. (15 ml) butter
3 tbsp. (45 ml) mayonnaise
1 tbsp. (15 ml) tarragon
1 tsp. (5 ml) thyme
1/2 tsp. (2 ml) salt
1/2 tsp. (2 ml) pepper
3 c. (750 ml) soft bread crumbs

- Clean salmon. Removal of the head is optional. I find it's too long with the head on.
- To remove the bones, use a boning knife, or one with a thin blade, and work with your fingers to slide the blade from the fish's spine, close to the bones, between the flesh and the bones.
- Continue to work with your fingers and the blade, slicing between the bones and the meat, from the spine outwards, from the head to the tail. Use the bone for a fish stock or throw it away.
- Chop a couple stalks of celery and an onion and saute in melted butter in a large pan until soft, then remove from heat.
- Combine mayonnaise with chopped fresh tarragon, thyme, salt and fresh-ground pepper. Add to vegetables and mix well.
- Add soft bread crumbs and combine well.
- Thoroughly grease a piece of sturdy foil large enough to completely cover the fish, then lay the salmon on one side of it.
- Stuff salmon. It doesn't matter if it won't close.
- Use a butcher's wrap to enclose the salmon in the foil, making sure it's all well-greased where it will touch the fish, or you'll lose the skin.
- Lay on a hot barbecue, fold side down and cook for about 10 minutes, with the barbecue lid down.
- Carefully turn over, using thick oven mitts, and continue to barbecue for about 15-20 minutes more, reducing the heat to moderate if your barbecue is very hot. Check to see if it's cooked through, but still nice and moist. Put the tip of a sharp knife into the thickest part and see if the flesh is opaque.
- Carefully transfer to a serving dish, removing foil everywhere but underneath the fish.
- Delicious cold too.
- Serves 10 or so.

WINE FOR STUFFED BARBECUED SALMON: *Pinot Noir is perfect and there are so many great ones in B.C. (Foxtrot, Quails' Gate, CedarCreek, Peller, Mt. Lehman, Alderlea). If you prefer a white, try Viognier (La Frenz, Poplar Grove, Cassini Cellars) or Marsanne (Inniskillin Okanagan, Moon Curser).*

Skewers of Barbecued Prawns

These are spicy and buttery and just delicious done on the barbecue. With the shells on, it's a bit messy to eat each, but the shells impart a terrific seafood flavour to the meat inside. Local spot prawns are usually available for a few weeks beginning in May, but they're also available frozen.

1 lb. (454 g) B.C. spot prawns

MARINADE:
2 garlic cloves
1 tbsp. (15 ml) ginger
1 tbsp. (15 ml) lemon juice
1 tsp. (5 ml) lemon zest
1/2 tsp. (2 ml) rosemary
1/2 tsp. (2 ml) thyme
1/2 tsp. (2 ml) cayenne pepper
1/4 tsp. (1 ml) black pepper
1/4 tsp. (1 ml) paprika
4 drops hot pepper sauce
2 tbsp. (30 ml) butter
2 tbsp. (30 ml) olive oil

- Rinse and slit prawns down the middle for easy peeling after cooking. Drain.
- Prepare marinade by mincing garlic and ginger; zesting lemon and mincing fresh and crumbling dried herbs.
- Melt butter in olive oil in small heavy pot over medium heat. Add all remaining ingredients and stir well. Bring to bubbling and cook gently for a few minutes before removing from the heat.
- When cool, pour a little more than half the seasoned butter over the prawns and combine well to coat each one. Marinate in the fridge for up to one hour.
- Thread onto skewers so they lay flat, using an even number for the number of people you wish to serve.
- Barbecue for about two or three minutes a side, until they all turn red from gray and are firm. Don't overcook.
- Serve with re-heated, reserved, seasoned butter alongside the prawns, and with a wedge of lemon. Offer plenty of napkins.
- Yum.
- Serves 2-4.

See photograph on page **20**

WINE:
Pinot Gris is my choice. Try Sandhill, Tinhorn Creek, Nichol Vineyard, Kettle Valley, Cerelia, Herder.

Barbecued Garlic Bread

These toasty slices of thick French bread are easy to make and will be everyone's favourite.

WINE FOR
BARBECUED
GARLIC BREAD:
*This calls for an
apple cider.*

2 garlic cloves
1/4 c. (60 ml) parmesan
2 tbsp. (30 ml) butter
4 slices French bread
1 tbsp. (15 ml) sesame seeds

- Mince garlic and combine with grated parmesan cheese and softened butter. Spread lightly on both sides of thick slices of French or Italian bread.
- Barbecue slices until nice and brown over medium heat, sprinkling with sesame seeds halfway through.
- Serves 4.

3. Easter Hams & Lambs

EASTER EGGS

My Mom always used to say "chicken eggs before chocolate ones" on Easter morning. What a spoilsport, I'd think.

But, then I caught myself repeating the same endearing admonition to my own kids. They were not impressed either – but I bet they repeat it to their kids today.

If that's the rule on Easter morning in your house, make it local eggs with a special twist, since it's a special morning. Whip them into an omelette, complete with a variety of favourite fillings.

You can stuff them with cream cheese and fresh spinach, chunky tomato sauce and local cheeses, mushrooms and bacon bits, the first local asparagus and ham or local herbs with cream cheese. You could also put seafood or fresh fruit or jam in it.

In Italy, it's called a frittata and the final step is to pop it under a broiler to set the surface. It often has fresh herbs, cheese, sometimes finely-sliced zucchini or spinach in it.

In China, it's egg foo yong and includes bean sprouts, mushrooms and greens, sometimes meat and green onions, and a soy-based sauce on the side.

In Germany, it's made with onions, bacon and potatoes, diced and cooked in the pan first, then beaten eggs are poured over top.

The French pour beaten eggs into a hot pan sizzling with a bit of butter. As the custard on top thickens and the bottom sets, the edge is carefully lifted, the pan tilted and the top runs under the bottom of the omelette to cook. One side is dabbed with a filling, then the other side folded over the top of the filling.

Then, there's the fluffy omelette which I've always felt was a bit of a nuisance to make, but delicious. It involves separating the eggs, whipping the whites to the soft peak stage, then folding them into the well-beaten yolks with a bit of salt and pepper, herbs or other seasonings. It's cooked in lots of melted butter; continuously folding the outer edges into the middle until it begins to set. The pan is then covered with a lid, or it's finished in the oven. It's Served flat, not folded, with a sprinkle of cheese for a light and fluffy confection.

Omelettes are best made in small batches rather than trying to make a six-egger and cutting it into slices. If all your ingredients are prepared ahead of time it's quick and easy to whip up a one or two-egger, then make another before that one's begun to cool.

It also allows everyone to choose their fillings.

I first learned to make a French omelette from a chef I worked for in my teens. Today, though, with the wonderful heavy non-stick cookware available, anyone can make a one-egg omelette in a six-inch pan with very little fuss, by just flipping the omelette before filling and folding.

Omelettes are substantial enough food to make a fine dinner or lunch as well as breakfast. It just depends on what you decide to fill them with.

Spinach & Cream Cheese Omelette

This is as simple, but nutritious and delicious a combination as you'll find and it makes a simple, quick breakfast or brunch.

1 egg
handful of fresh spinach leaves
1/2 tsp. (2 ml) butter
2 tbsp. (30 ml) cream cheese
salt and pepper to taste

- Beat egg with a wisk.
- Just wilt the spinach in a glass bowl in the microwave.
- Heat a wee dab of butter in a heavy six-inch non-stick pan over medium heat until melted and sizzling, but not browned.
- Pour in the egg and swirl it to cover the bottom.
- When the bottom is set, (lift a bit with the spatula) gently flip it over and lower the heat.
- Immediately dab and spread the cream cheese (regular or low fat) over half the omelette and arrange the spinach over top.
- Sprinkle salt and pepper over it, and fold the other half over the filling.
- Leave it for a few seconds more until the cream cheese begins to melt, then slide onto a plate.
- Serves 1.

Ham & Greens with Rice

This is simple, nutritious, but a delicious meal in one bowl which also heats up beautifully. Great for using up the last of the ham. Use any kind of mild greens, from spinach to collards.

1 lb. (454 g) greens
1 onion
1/2 c. (125 ml) chopped ham
2 c. (500 ml) chicken broth
1 c. (250 ml) long grain white rice
pinch of cayenne pepper
fresh ground pepper

- Wash greens well and chop finely. Dice onion and chop ham into small dice.
- If home made stock is not available, use a better quality, lower salt version of prepared stock, because the flavour is important.
- Combine all ingredients in a large pot and bring to bubbling. Reduce heat, cover and simmer for 20 minutes, or until all liquid has been absorbed.
- Serves 2 to 3.

WINE WITH EGGS:
Matching wine with eggs is tough but thank heaven for the versatility of sparkling wine. Good choices include Sumac Ridge Steller's Jay, Cipes Brut, Gray Monk Odyssey Brut and, on Vancouver Island, Venturi-Schulze Brut Natural or Starling Lane's Célébration Brut.

WINE FOR HAM & GREENS WITH RICE:
This calls for a dry rosé like Venturi-Schulze's Rosso di Collina or Domaine de Chaberton's North Bluff Pink, a Zinfandel rosé..

Egg Foo Yung with Greens

This crisp and fresh-tasting way to serve eggs could be a light meal or a hearty breakfast. Add fresh little baby shrimp to it for something really special.

1 c. (250 ml) fresh bean sprouts
5 mushrooms
2 c. (500 ml) greens
3 eggs
2 tsp. (10 ml) olive oil

- Rinse a handful of bean sprouts in cold water, drain and pat dry.
- Clean mushrooms and cut into small dice.
- Wash and chop greens of your choice such as spinach, arugula or a mesclun mix.
- Lightly beat eggs in a large bowl and add vegetables. Mix.
- Heat oil or melt butter in a non-stick pan, and pour spoonfuls of the egg and vegetable mixture in, just as you would make pancakes.
- Let each little omelette brown for a minute or so before turning and browning the other side. They can be made any size you like.
- Keep warm while you make up the rest of them.

SAUCE:
1 tbsp. (15 ml) cold water
2 tsp. (10 ml) cornstarch
1/2 c. (125 ml) chicken stock
2 tsp. (10 ml) soy sauce

- Dissolve cornstarch in cold water in a small bowl and set aside.
- Bring stock to a boil in a small pot and add soy sauce. Stir in re-combined cornstarch mixture, stirring constantly.
- When bubbling, thickened and clear, just keep the sauce warm until ready to serve.
- Add salt only if needed.
- Drizzle a bit of sauce over each omelette.
- Serves 4.

See photograph on page 37

TOP:
**Egg Foo
Yung with
Greens**

Recipe on
page **36**

BOTTOM:
**Winnie's
Nest Eggs**

Recipe on
page **41**

TOP:
**Easter
Bunny
Cake**
Recipe on
page **43**

BOTTOM:
**Spinach &
Ham Sauce**
Recipe on
page **44**

TOP:
Spinach Pie

Recipe on
page **50**

BOTTOM:
Fluffy Yogurt Pancakes

Recipe on
page **55**

TOP:
**Feta &
Strawberry
Salad**

Recipe on
page **59**

BOTTOM:
**Shortcut
Shortcakes**

Recipe on
page **59**

Winnie's Nest Eggs for a Bunch

This is a great recipe for when you have a bunch of people to serve breakfast to, especially if they're in a hurry to get to the Easter Egg Hunt. This can be varied to your taste by substituting other types of luncheon meat for the ham slices. You can leave out the spinach, and you could substitute cheddar or other cheese for the Swiss, too.

6 ham slices
12 spinach leaves
6 eggs
1/2 c. (125 ml) Swiss cheese
6 English muffins

WINE:
This calls for a red sparkling wine like Oak Bay Northern Lights or Cipes Rosé

- Pre-heat oven to 350 F.
- Form a deep cup with the ham or other meat in muffin tins, add the spinach, then break an egg into it.
- Sprinkle the top with grated cheese and bake for 14 minutes for soft-cooked eggs, more for hard-cooked.
- The timing and oven temperature are critical if you're fussy about how well done your eggs are. Check a couple of minutes earlier by pressing the white near the yolk to see how well-cooked the eggs are. Remove just before they firm up because they continue to cook after being removed from the oven.
- Serve on toasted English muffins.
- Serves 3 to 6.

See photograph on page 37

Chocolate Easter Egg Nests

These are so cute you can use them for an edible centrepiece or for place names at each setting for your Easter dinner. Just make small ones and poke a wooden skewer into the chocolate before it hardens so you can write guests' names on a piece of paper to glue to the stick.

4 squares semi-sweet chocolate
3 c. (750 ml) dried chowmein noodles
jelly beans or candy-coated chocolate
    Easter eggs

- Melt chocolate in a metal bowl over hot water, or on medium in the microwave oven in a glass bowl for about two minutes, then stir for a minute or two until all the chocolate is melted.
- Add dried chow mein noodles and stir well so all the noodles are coated with chocolate.
- Working fairly quickly so the chocolate doesn't harden before you have formed the nests, dump large spoonfuls of the mix onto wax paper, then form nests by using forks or fingers to create a hollow in the middle and pushing the sides in and up to form the rim of the nest.
- Imagine birds' nests and remember it doesn't have to be perfectly smooth, but the 'sticks' do need to be close enough together for the chocolate to bind it all together.
- Put in the refrigerator for 5 minutes or so while the chocolate hardens, then fill the nests with colourful candy eggs.
- Makes four medium or six smaller nests.

WINE FOR CHOCOLATE EASTER EGG NESTS:
Serve a big red like a Seven Stones Cabernet Franc or an Inniskillin Dark Horse Vineyard Cabernet Sauvignon; or with Rustic Roots unique Mulberry Pear dessert wine.

Easter Bunny Cake

You know how bunny rabbits have a reputation for reproducing prolifically? Well, that can happen with this cake, too. I made one and ended up with two. The icing is sickly sweet, but the kids just love it – big ones and little ones.

1 Devil's food cake mix
1/2 c. (125 ml) coconut
a few black and pink jelly beans
a few white marshmallows

PAT'S FLUFFY ICING:
2 unbeaten egg whites
1 c. (250 ml) white sugar
1/3 c. (75 ml) water
1/4 tsp. (1 ml) cream of tartar
pinch of salt
1 tsp. (5 ml) vanilla

■ Make the cake according to package instructions, in two eight-inch round cake pans, and let it cool. You could use any flavour of cake you like, or you can make your favourite from scratch instead of using a cake mix. I used chocolate.

■ Prepare the fur by toasting the coconut in a 300 F oven for about 15 minutes, or until nicely browned.

■ To make the icing: separate the eggs and put the whites into a large glass bowl.

■ Heat sugar, water, cream of tartar and salt in a pot until boiling. Turn off the heat.

■ Begin to beat the egg whites, very gradually adding the hot syrup and beating on high speed until very stiff. Add the vanilla and beat it in at the end.

■ Spread icing between the layers, flat sides together, then use a serrated knife to cut the cake in half. Set each half on its cut side on a plate, then carve off a thin wedge at one end, to flatten the mound there a bit. That will be the bunny's face.

■ Frost the bunny's sides, top and back thickly with the fluffy icing, then the face. Scatter toasted coconut all over it.

■ Push a whole marshmallow into the icing at the bottom end for a tail.

■ You may want to practice with the marshmallows on a board or plate before selecting the ones for the face. I used one, cut in half and squeezed to elongate it, for each ear. To make them longer, I cut one into a point, then removed a vee notch from the other, so the point fit snugly into the notch to make a larger ear than a single marshmallow would.

■ Cut another marshmallow in half for the cheeks.

■ Use dark brown or black jelly beans for eyes and pink ones for the nose and a mouth.

■ You'll find after you've practised on one, you can eat it, and make another with the other half of the cake.

See photograph on page **38**

Ham & Potato Scallop

This is a great way to make a second meal with leftover ham, or you could purchase slices to make this easy one-dish meal as a simpler Easter ham dinner for one or two.

2 large potatoes
1 onion
1 c. (250 ml) chopped ham
2 tbsp. (30 ml) butter
2 tbsp. (30 ml) flour
salt and pepper to taste
1 1/4 c. (310 ml) milk

- Pre-heat oven to 350F.
- Wash and thinly slice unpeeled potatoes, arranging a layer in a large greased casserole dish.
- Cover with a layer of thinly-sliced onion, then chopped slices of ham.
- Dot with bits of butter, sprinkle with flour, then another layer of potatoes.
- Continue with onion, ham, butter and flour until your ingredients are all used up, finishing with a layer of potato slices.
- Add salt and pepper to milk and pour it evenly over the top.
- Cover and bake for about a half hour, then uncover to cook for a further 30 minutes to one hour.
- Serves 4 to 6.

Spinach & Ham Sauce

This is a favourite of our family, and a fabulous way to use the last bits of ham left on the bone before it goes into the soup pot. It could be served over rice, pasta or even toast; or as the filling for something like crepes as a special dinner.

2 c. (500 ml) white sauce
1 bunch spinach
1 c. (250 ml) ham dice
2 green onions
1/4 c. (60 ml) Swiss cheese
1/4 tsp. (1 ml) nutmeg
1/8 tsp. (.5 ml) white pepper
salt to taste

- Use any recipe to make up a medium white sauce in a fairly large bowl. (I usually make it in the microwave).
- Wash, stem and chop fresh spinach, or you could thaw a package of frozen spinach.
- Add it to the hot white sauce and cook it for a minute or so, whisking well.
- Add a cup or so of finely chopped ham, and a couple of minced green onions, grated Swiss cheese, nutmeg, white pepper and salt, whisking and cooking until the ham is heated through.

See photograph on page **38**

WINE FOR HAM & POTATO SCALLOP: *This calls for blended red wine with no pretentions, just lots of flavour, like Robin Ridge's Robin's Return or Summerhill's Baco Noir.*

Mom's Crepes

These are light and delicious. A non-stick six or seven-inch frypan works well for making crepes. My favourite filling uses up the bits left over from a ham dinner. (See Ham & Spinach Sauce on page 44.)

1 1/2 c. (375 ml) flour
1 tsp. (5 ml) baking powder
1 tsp. (5 ml) salt
12 oz. (355 ml) beer
1 1/4 c. (310) water
3 eggs
3 tbsp. (45 ml) butter

WINE FOR MOM'S CREPES:
It all depends on the filling. With Judie's ham filling, I recommend a Pinot Noir rosé from Mistaken Identity Vineyards, or a Gamay Noir from Beaumont, both organic producers.

- Mix dry ingredients. Stir in beer and water, beating until fairly smooth. Add eggs and melted butter and beat again.
- Let batter stand for 10 minutes while you make the filling.
- Lightly grease frypan and heat on high.
- Use about a quarter cup of batter to make six-inch crepes, just covering the bottom of the pan, and swirling it to assure even coverage of the pan.
- As soon as the edges begin to dry, turn the crepe with a smooth motion of the flipper. Don't turn until the bottom is cooked all over or it'll tear.
- Cook for another couple of minutes before slipping out onto a warmed platter, kept in a warm oven.
- Makes 16 or so, enough for four or more.
- Halve the recipe for two, or double it and freeze the crepes, separating them with plastic wrap, wax paper or parchment paper for later use.

Stuffed Easter Lamb Roll

The stuffing is a combination of flavours that are excellent with fresh B.C. lamb, and it looks very festive when it comes out of the oven. Because the bulgur is less rich than a bread base, it's a good choice for a lamb stuffing. You could use a boneless lamb leg or shoulder roast for this.

2 lb. (1 kg) boneless lamb

MARINADE:
2 tbsp. (30 ml) dry white wine
1 lemon rind
1 tbsp. (15 ml) olive oil
2 garlic cloves
1 tsp. (5 ml) tarragon
1/2 tsp. (2 ml) thyme
1/2 tsp. (2 ml) black pepper

STUFFING:
2 c. (500 ml) spinach
4 dried apricots
3 tbsp. (45 ml) camembert cheese
1 tbsp. (15 ml) fresh mint
1/2 c. (125 ml) bulgur
1 c. (250 ml) water
1/2 tsp. (2 ml) sea salt

- Trim fat from the lamb. (A little cap of fat could be left on the top of the roll.)
- Zest the lemon and mince it and the garlic.
- Combine all marinade ingredients and turn the boneless lamb roast about in the marinade so it's completely glazed with it. Refrigerate overnight or for as long as possible the day of cooking.
- Finely chop fresh spinach, dried apricots, camembert and fresh mint.
- Combine bulgur with a cup of water and simmer on low for about 15 minutes.
- Remove from heat and immediately add pieces of camembert, mixing so it melts into the grain.
- Add remaining ingredients and mix well.
- Lay lamb out on wax paper and spread stuffing all over the meat. Roll up and secure with a skewer or two, or tie with butcher's twine.
- Set in a roasting pan and drizzle with the remaining marinade, if there's any left.
- Roast in a 350 F oven for about 25 minutes to the pound.
- Serves 4 to 6.

WINE FOR STUFFED EASTER LAMB ROLL: *This is Easter – break the bank for one of the many red icon wines such as Laughing Stock's Portolio, Mission Hill's Quatrain, Church & State's Quintessential, Black Widow's Hourglass, Howling Bluff's Sin Cera.*

Seafood & Cheese Sauce

This is delicate and delicious. You could use shrimp, crab or scallops, cut into small pieces, or add chopped, browned mushrooms for a different flavor.

1/3 lb. (150 g) shrimp
2 c. (500 ml) white sauce
1/2 c. (125 ml) Swiss cheese
2 green onions
1 tsp. (5 ml) lemon juice
1/2 tsp. (2 ml) tarragon
1/8 tsp (.5 ml) white pepper
salt to taste

WINE FOR SEAFOOD & CHEESE SAUCE: *There are lots of options: Pinot Gris, Le Vieux Pin's Petit Blanc; a dry Gewürztraminer (such as Arrowleaf) or a dry Ortega, such as Starling Lane or Larch Hills.*

- Rinse fresh shrimp, scallops, crab or mushrooms and set aside to drain. If using mushrooms, brown lightly in a little butter.
- Use any recipe to make up a medium white sauce.
- Add grated cheese to the hot sauce, stirring it in until it melts.
- Mince green onions and add, along with lemon juice, tarragon and white pepper.
- Add seafood or mushrooms and lightly stir in, then cook for a minute or so to warm everything through.
- Taste for seasoning.

4. Mom's & Victoria's Days

FIST FOOD FOR OUTDOORS

Weather aside, this is the time of year to take your food outside – and I don't mean out onto the deck.

This Victoria Day pack the cooler or picnic basket, the back pack or your pockets, and go for a ramble, a walk, a hike, a trek, a drive or a ride.

There's nothing like a meal beside a bubbling stream, overlooking a lake or the ocean, amongst the wildflowers or underneath towering evergreens.

The herbaceous smell of crushed plants; fresh, icy water tumbling down from snowfields high above; the salty tang of an ocean breeze and even dust muddied by early summer rain are all smells of outdoors that no air freshener can emulate.

Food tastes better outside. Or is it just that you're hungrier after a bit of exercise and fresh air?

Whatever the reason, take advantage of that, and pack a lunch. And not just sandwiches.

Pack leftovers, but not just any leftovers: make carefully planned meals with the next day's picnic in mind.

Chicken's easy because any leftover bits are great cold, but the best parts are drumsticks, which come complete with handles for easy munching on the trail.

For something a bit more sophisticated, try an easy finger-food luncheon with a Mediterranean twist.

Next time you barbecue, cook a couple of chicken skewers on one side of the grill, along with dinner. Pop them into the fridge and take them with you, cold, on your picnic a day or so later.

Add some fresh colourful sweet local peppers, a nice tangy dip, and you've got lunch.

Don't bother with a mess of cutlery. Just use your handy Swiss Army knife to slice pieces off whole peppers to scoop up some yogurt dip.

An excellent addition would be fresh little whole wheat pita breads, or a dish of cold bulgur seasoned with fresh mint and parsley from the garden, and a little fresh lemon juice and olive oil (see Tabouleh). A fork may be needed for the bulgur, but you could also tear off bits of pita bread to scoop it up.

Picnics don't have to be a lot of mess and bother. They can be simple and still be fun. So pack your picnic bag, grab your sweetie and off you go.

Because the British Queen Victoria's birthday was May 24, the Monday preceding May 25 each year has been a statutory holiday called Victoria Day in Canada since 1952, even though she died in 1901.

Rather than celebrating Victoria's birthday, it is now the date Canadians celebrate the birthday of the reigning monarch of the United Kingdom, even though the current Queen Elizabeth's birthday is actually April 21. Although Victoria Day is generally celebrated with festivals and fun events, often outdoors now, the long weekend is looked on by many as the first of the summer long weekends.

Chicken Souvlaki

These skewered cubes of grilled meat are delectable cold as well as hot off the grill. If chicken's scarce, try it with pork or beef, or prawns.

4 boneless chicken thighs
1/2 lemon
1 garlic clove
1 tbsp. (15 ml) fresh parsley
1 tsp. (5 ml) fresh oregano
1 tsp. (5 ml) olive oil

- Soak bamboo kebab skewers in cold water for a half hour or so.
- Skin thighs, trim meat of fat and cut into chunks about one inch square.
- Zest lemon, mince it, then juice the lemon; squish or chop garlic; and chop herbs.
- Combine all ingredients in a glass bowl with the chicken and let marinate for an hour or so before threading onto soaked bamboo skewers which have been rubbed with a smidge of cooking oil.
- Barbecue for about 15 minutes, turning until all sides are nicely browned but the meat is not dried out.
- Be careful the wooden skewers are not over the flame.
- Cool and refrigerate until you're ready to assemble your picnic food.
- Serves 2.

WINE FOR CHICKEN SOUVLAKI:
This calls for a full-flavoured white like a Gewürztraminer from Arrowleaf, Gray Monk, Thornhaven, Dirty Laundry or Sumac Ridge.

Yogurt & Herb Dip

This is great with barbecued chicken, pork or beef, raw sweet peppers and onions or other raw vegetables. There's no fat. At this time of year the fresh herbs like chives are at their best from the garden, so feature them in special dishes.

1/4 c. (60 ml) skim yogurt
1 tbsp. (15 ml) fresh chives
2 tsp. (10 ml) fresh parsley
1/4 tsp. (1 ml) sugar
salt and pepper to taste

- Chop fresh herbs finely and combine with other ingredients.

Feta Spread or Dip

This is great on crackers, pita crisps, fresh pita triangles or chunks of fresh sweet local peppers.

1/2 c. (125 ml) feta
1/4 c. (60 ml) red onion
3 tbsp. (45 ml) fresh parsley
1 tbsp. (15 ml) fresh oregano
1 tbsp. (15 ml) olive oil
2 tsp. (10 ml) lemon juice
salt and pepper to taste

- Crumble feta cheese and very finely chop red onion.
- Chop herbs.
- Toss all ingredients together with the olive oil and lemon juice.
- Add salt and pepper to taste.
- Top crackers or pita bread with this, or scoop up a bite with pita crisps.

Spinach Pie

This delectable, light and crisp cheesy pie is a classic Greek dish called Spanakopita. The filling can also be enclosed in layers of filo pastry and rolled up in a triangular shape for individual pies.

1 onion
1 garlic clove
drizzle of oil
1 1/2 lb. (675 g) spinach
1/2 lb. (227 g) feta cheese
1/4 c. (60 ml) Swiss cheese
3 eggs
1/2 c. (125 ml) fresh parsley
1/4 c. (60 ml) fresh mint or dill
1/4 tsp. (1 ml) nutmeg
salt and pepper, to taste
1 lb. (454 g) filo pastry
1/4 c. (60 ml) butter
2 tbsp. (30 ml) olive oil

- Pre-heat oven to 350 F.
- Chop onion and mince garlic.
- Heat a drizzle of oil on medium heat in a large pan. (I use a big wok if using fresh spinach).
- Saute onions until soft and beginning to brown lightly. Add garlic and soften it too.
- Thaw frozen spinach if using; chop fresh and wilt in the pan with the onions and garlic.
- Remove from heat and let cool while you crumble the feta, grate the Swiss cheese and beat the eggs in a small bowl.
- Mince fresh herbs and add the cheeses, eggs, herbs and seasonings to the onion and spinach mixture and combine well.
- Melt the butter and olive oil.
- Unroll the filo pastry and dampen a tea towel to cover it and keep it from drying out as you assemble the pie.
- Lightly spray a rectangular pan, 8x12 inches or so, and lay the first sheet of filo in the bottom. Brush it with melted butter and oil, then repeat with four or five more sheets. Top with half the filling.
- Repeat with another half a dozen sheets, brushing each lightly with butter, and spread the remainder of the filling on top.
- Finish with the remainder of the package of filo pastry sheets, brushing the top with the last of the melted butter.
- Bake for about 40 minutes, or until top browns.
- You may also cut the filo sheets into strips and wrap a spoonful of filling into a triangle, for appetizer spinach pies.
- Serves at least 6 for dinner, more as an appetizer.

See photograph on page **39**

WINE FOR SPINACH PIE:
A crisp white is made to order with this – such as the Lake Breeze Pinot Blanc or Nk'Mip Pinot Blanc.

Vietnamese Salad Rolls

Most of the ingredients for these can now be purchased at larger supermarkets, but they're certainly available at specialty grocery stores featuring Oriental foods.

They have a light, delicate flavor, while the sauce for dipping is stronger flavoured by contrast. The exotic combination of peanut butter, spice and sweetness tickles the tastebuds.

These are a bit of a nuisance to make, but well worth it, and they can be made up earlier in the day and kept in the fridge ready to serve when you want. You could use cold, cooked chicken or pork, crab, lobster, shrimp or a substitute.

8 rounds of rice paper
8 oz. (225 g) vermicelli
8 green onions
8 lettuce leaves
8 oz. (225 g) chicken or seafood

- If using the smaller (8-inch) rice paper rounds, make twice as many salad rolls, and if the green onions are large, cut length-wise in half, to match the rice paper.
- Bring a pot of water to a boil and turn it off. Add rice or bean thread vermicelli noodles and let soak for five minutes or so. Rinse with cold water and drain well.
- Fill a large bowl or deep frypan (wide enough to hold a sheet of rice paper) with very warm water. Have all ingredients within reach.

- Immerse one sheet of rice paper in the hot water for a few seconds, until it softens enough to handle. Lift and drain, then lay on your work surface and fold up the bottom third.
- Lay a leaf of lettuce on the folded part, then arrange an ounce of noodles lengthwise on top.
- Fold sides of rice paper in over noodles, then arrange a piece of seafood or meat in front of the lettuce and noodles.
- Set a blade of green onion in front so it will stick out from the salad roll, then roll up snugly, enclosing everything inside.
- Continue until everything's used up, arranging attractively on a serving plate.
- Makes 16 small or eight large salad rolls.

DIPPING SAUCE:
1/4 c. (60 ml) chili sauce
1 tbsp. (15 ml) crunchy peanut butter
1/4 c. (60 ml) hoisin sauce
2 tbsp. (30 ml) water
fresh cilantro to garnish

- Mix everything together thoroughly, adding a bit more water if needed so it is the right consistency to dip.
- Serve alongside the rolls for dipping.

WINE FOR VIETNAMESE SALAD ROLLS: *I would start with something with a little natural sweetness, like the Schönburger-Gewürztraminer or Desert Sun from Gehringer Brothers, to flatter the Thai flavours.*

MOM'S 'IT' IN MAY

Mother's Day is a great excuse for treating your favourite mom, whether it's your own mother, your wife, a friend or a relative, to something special on that day. Be warned, it'll make you feel good too.

As with most occasions, food is a great way to show you care.

While the cook for Mother's Day feasts is frequently not the most experienced one in the household, there's always lots of love that goes into the meal. And, that's the most important ingredient of all.

The act of preparing something to eat for someone you love is really why home cooking is so revered.

There are lots of recipes for simply-made dishes which are just as yummy as those that are much more difficult to make.

For instance, when it comes to salads, there are some excellent, prepared greens available now which need little more than a bright addition or two and a garnish, before they're wrapped in a simple dressing and topped with some toasted nuts.

I have fuzzy memories from when I was a kid, of slipping out of bed Mother's Day morning and tiptoeing into the kitchen, sliding the door closed, and setting to work preparing breakfast for Mom.

Dusting and tidying up the living room were a couple of other surprises she really appreciated, so I'd try to do that silently, without breaking anything, before she woke.

Then I'd sneak out into her beautiful garden and collect a posy to put into a vase for her.

Some years I'd gather those wild spring sunflowers that dot the Okanagan hills, and I remember they always made their way back outdoors before the day was done. I think they were full of bugs.

But, Moms aren't fussy about how perfect whatever you prepare for them is. It's usually enough that you went to the trouble to do it.

Since I became a mom myself, Mother's Day has been my opportunity to spend hours getting dirt under my nails in the garden, without having to worry about what we'll have for dinner, followed by a lovely get-together with my family around the table – and that seems just about perfect to me.

I hope yours is too.

Chive & Cheddar Muffins

If you don't have a muffin tin, these can be baked in spoonfuls dropped on a greased cookie sheet, but reduce the cooking time slightly. Fresh chives from the garden are perfect early in spring, and perhaps Mom would be tickled by a glass of sparkling wine served alongside these for brunch.

2 tbsp. (30 ml) chives
1 1/2 c. (375 ml) flour
1/2 c. (125 ml) whole wheat flour
4 tsp. (20 ml) baking powder
1 tbsp. (15 ml) brown sugar
1/2 tsp. (2 ml) salt
2 c. (500 ml) grated cheddar
2 eggs
1 c. (250 ml) milk
3 tbsp. (45 ml) melted butter

- Pre-heat oven to 425F.
- Cut chives from the garden, then snip them into little bits.
- Combine dry ingredients. You could substitute a quarter cup of oat bran or cornmeal for some of the white flour for added crunch and nutrition.
- When thoroughly blended, mix in the chopped chives.
- Grate cheddar and combine all but a quarter cup or so with the dry ingredients. Set the remainder aside to sprinkle on top just before baking.
- Beat eggs, milk and melted butter together in a small bowl or measuring cup.
- Combine wet and dry ingredients, mixing briefly, just until blended.
- Divide amongst 12 greased muffin tins, then sprinkle cheese on top.
- Bake in a hot oven for 20 minutes or so, until browned.

Yogurt Waffles

This is quite a thick batter, but it results in a very crisp, airy waffle. I use fat-free yogurt and it doesn't harm the end result, but you could even substitute sour cream if you like.

2 eggs
1 c. (250 ml) plain yogurt
1/2 c. (125 ml) oil
1 1/2 c. (375 ml) flour
1 tbsp. (15 ml) baking powder
1 tsp. (5 ml) baking soda
1/4 tsp. (1 ml) salt

- Beat eggs and add yogurt, combining well in a large measuring cup or bowl. (The large measuring cups have a spout, so are great to use to just pour a gob of batter on the hot waffle iron).
- Add all the rest of the ingredients, beating until the batter is smooth.
- Follow the directions which came with your waffle iron for baking, but don't use too much batter or it'll squish out the sides and make a mess.
- For breakfast you could lay a thinly-sliced piece of bacon on top of the batter before baking.
- For dessert waffles or brunch you could garnish with a spoonful of fresh or frozen berries or fruit, which have been chopped and warmed slightly over medium heat. (see Merry Berries).

Merry Berries

These are delicious over crisp waffles or pancakes for breakfast or dessert, or over ice cream, custard, angel food cake or a meringue. As fresh B.C. berries such as strawberries, raspberries and blueberries become available, include them. You could also try some fresh Okanagan cherries, peaches, nectarines or even pears in this.

1 c. (250 ml) strawberries
1 c. (250 ml) other berries
1 tbsp. (15 ml) cognac
1 tsp. (5 ml) honey
1/4 tsp. (1 ml) allspice

- Rinse and chop fresh berries, other fruit, or a combination of fresh and frozen fruits.
- Crush them slightly to release some juice.
- Add remaining ingredients and mix well. (You can omit the cognac or substitute brandy or another liqueur).
- Let it sit while you prepare the base, whether that's waffles, angel food cake or whatever.
- Serves 2-6.

Fluffy Yogurt Pancakes

These can be made with or without fruit in them. I have made them with blueberries I froze fresh from the Fraser Valley in the summer. They rise beautifully and are as light and fluffy as can be. You could substitute all white or whole wheat flour for the oat bran, or cornmeal.

WINE FOR FLUFFY YOGURT PANCAKES:
It is sparkling wine with the waffles and the pancakes.

1/4 c. (60 ml) flour
1/4 c. (60 ml) oat bran
1/4 c. (60 ml) whole wheat flour
1 tbsp. (15 ml) sugar
2 tsp. (10 ml) baking powder
1/2 tsp. (3 ml) baking soda
1/2 tsp. (3 ml) salt
2 eggs
1 c. (250 ml) plain yogurt
3/4 c. (175 ml) blueberries

- Combine dry ingredients in a bowl with a whisk until well mixed and make a well in the centre.
- Beat eggs slightly in another bowl with the whisk and add the yogurt (I use fat-free) and mix well. Combine the wet and dry ingredients together, then fold in fruit such as blueberries, if you wish.
- Heat a heavy, cast iron pan or your favourite pancake frypan over medium to medium-high heat and drizzle a little cooking oil over the surface. Add a small dab of butter for flavour.
- Drop the thick batter by spoonfuls onto the sizzling surface, turning when they've risen nicely and the underside is browned.
- Brown the other side well before removing to a serving plate.
- Add another drizzle of oil and a wee dab of butter to the pan for each batch.
- Serves 2 or 3.

See photograph on page **39**

Garlic Butter Prawns in Wine

This is very easy to make and would convince any mother of your devotion, I'm sure. We developed this recipe after trying a prawn dish we loved at an Italian restaurant many years ago.It has been refined over the years, but continues to be a favourite in our home whenever we can get fresh, B.C. spot prawns, or frozen ones. You can adjust the seasonings to your taste.

1 tbsp. (15 ml) ginger
1 large garlic clove
3 green onions
1/2 lb. (250 g) spot prawns
1 tbsp. (15 ml) olive oil
1 lemon, juiced
1/4 tsp. (1 ml) chili powder
1/4 tsp. (1 ml) cayenne
1 tbsp. (15 ml) butter
    1/2 c. (125 ml) white wine

- Mince ginger and garlic and finely chop green onions.
- Prepare fresh prawns by removing the head, rinsing well in cold water and slitting the shells. That makes it easier to remove the meat from the shells later. Cooking them in their shells makes them messier to eat, but really adds a distinctive prawn flavour to the dish.
- (Remove them if you don't want to get your fingers too greasy.)
- Warm olive oil over medium-high heat in a cast iron frypan and toss in the ginger, garlic and half the green onions.
- Stir about until sizzling well, then add the juice of one lemon, chili powder, cayenne and butter.
- When all is bubbling, add the prawns, turning over after a couple of minutes, and adding the wine.
- Adjust the heat to keep everything sizzling nicely, and cook for just a few minutes until the prawns have turned opaque and pink.
- Serve with a loaf of fresh, crusty French bread which can be torn into chunks to soak up the cooking sauce.
- Serves 4 as an appetizer.

WINE FOR GARLIC BUTTER PRAWNS IN WINE:
The first choice is the wine you cook with, perhaps a Viognier from Jackson-Triggs or Black Hills.

Summer

5. A Berry Nice Summer

SWEET SOLSTICE

June's Summer Solstice officially welcomes vacation season, so it's nice to have light, refreshing fare around for friends and family who drop by.

Summer is that yummy time of the year when berries and cherries are ripening in the fields and orchards of B.C.

A shortcake dessert may be the classic way to make use of the freshest berries of the year, but think outside the box.

Try berries in a salad of lovely fresh local greens, on your cereal in the morning, with yogurt and granola as a snack, in a compote with your main meal – or in your favourite dessert recipes.

Fresh strawberries and raspberries are delicious with a sharp cheese such as blue or feta, and they're a surprising treat in a salad, or with chicken or pork.

Okanagan cherries go deliciously with a roast duckling or game meats as well as in a pie or over ice cream.

Juicy blueberries take whole grains such as oats in muffins, coffee cakes, pancakes and cereal to a whole new level, and they're excellent squashed over a slice of lemon cheesecake.

There's a lot of talk about antioxidants in fruit and their role in preventing cancer. I don't know much about that, but I do know they're delicious, and they're at their very best in season, plucked right from the bush, tree or vine.

If you want to enjoy some of their wonderful flavours when the snow's on the ground and summer seems far away, turn them into jam or jelly to preserve them. Or, I like to freeze them on a cookie sheet, so the hard little icy pellets can be poured into a freezer bag. Later, I thaw as many as I want and toss a few into muffins and loaves or over cereal or yogurt.

Feta & Strawberry Salad

Mesclun is a lively mixture of edible leaves, including a variety of lettuces, spinach, arugula, young dandelion and lamb's quarters, mustard, kale, curly endive, watercress and chinese cabbage. Sometimes fresh herbs such as parsley and edible flowers such as calendula, chive flowers or rose and marigold petals are added.

4 c. (1 l) fresh greens
2 green onions
2 c. (500 ml) berries
1/4 c. (60 ml) crumbled feta
2 tbsp. (30 ml) chopped nuts
3 tbsp. (45 ml) balsamic vinegar
2 tbsp. (30 ml) olive oil
fresh ground black pepper

- Wash and tear greens into a large salad bowl and chop up the little green onions. If using strawberries, cut into raspberry-sized chunks, but leave raspberries or blueberries whole.
- Crumble feta over top, then chop nuts such as walnuts, pecans or almonds and garnish the salad with them.
- Whisk together oil and vinegar. Grind fresh pepper over the greens and berries then sprinkle them with the oil and vinegar dressing and serve.
- Serves 4.

See photograph on page **40**

WINE FOR FETA AND STRAWBERRY SALAD:
I have had great success in pairing salads with fruit wines, like the pear wines from Elephant Island or Sleeping Giant fruit wineries or apple-pear wine from Rustic Roots Winery.

Shortcut Shortcakes

These are super easy to make and soak up the berry juices beautifully. Just cut each biscuit in half and top with cut-up berries which have been sprinkled with a little sugar. (This helps to release their lovely juices.) Top with freshly-whipped cream and grated chocolate.

1 1/2 c. (375 ml) flour
1/2 c. (125 ml) whole wheat flour
3 tbsp. (45 ml) sugar
4 tsp. (20 ml) baking powder
1 tsp. (5 ml) salt
1/3 c. (75 ml) olive oil
3/4 c. (175 ml) milk
milk and sugar to garnish

- Pre-heat oven to 425 F.
- Combine the dry ingredients in a large bowl and blend well with a wire whisk.
- Add the liquid ingredients and stir with a wooden spoon until just mixed.
- Turn out onto a well-floured board and knead for a minute or two. Form with your hands or roll into one-inch thickness and cut biscuits the size you like, (a drinking glass works well in the absence of a biscuit-cutter) putting them onto an ungreased baking sheet.
- Brush the tops with milk and sprinkle with sugar, to garnish.
- Bake for about 15 minutes, or until browned.
- Makes about 8 shortcakes.

See photograph on page **40**

Creamy Berries with Nuts and Chocolate

This is a quick and easy dessert to make, but it's light and delicious and it looks inviting, too.

3 c. (750 ml) berries or cherries
1 1/2 c. (375 ml) plain yogurt
3 tbsp. (45 ml) brown sugar
2 tbsp. (30 ml) brandy
shaved chocolate
chopped roasted almonds
sprinkle of nutmeg

- Prepare fruit by hulling, pitting or stoning and cutting up larger fruit. Sprinkle with a bit of sugar if you wish.
- Thoroughly mix low-fat, plain yogurt with brown sugar and brandy, (you may substitute juice or a different liqueur) until it's well-mixed.
- Divide fruit amongst stemmed glass fruit dishes and top with a few dollops of the yogurt mixture.
- Garnish with chocolate, almonds and a sprinkle of nutmeg.
- Serves 6-8.

Raspberry Glaze

This is just bursting with raspberry flavour, but without those pesky seeds. Serve it over cheesecake, angel food cake, waffles, fruit salad or ice cream. In fact, it would probably be nice mixed with a little oil and vinegar for a salad dressing.

2 c. (500 ml) raspberries
1 tbsp. (15 ml) brown sugar
2 tbsp. (30 ml) cornstarch

- Squash raspberries and push through a fine sieve or food mill until you have two cups of fruit. Discard the seeds.
- Pour puree into a pot and dissolve brown sugar and cornstarch in the juice. Bring the mixture to bubbling over medium heat, stirring constantly, until it thickens slightly and clears.
- Remove from heat and cool completely.
- Refrigerate until ready to use.

WINE FOR RASPBERRY GLAZE: *Can you ever overdo the flavours of raspberry? I would serve this with a raspberry wine from The Fort Winery or MooBerry or Westham Island.*

Chocolate Raspberry Cheesecake

Raspberry season is the perfect time to indulge in one of my favourite flavour combinations: dark chocolate and raspberries. This recipe was adapted from one on the Oreo baking crumbs box.

CRUST:
1 1/4 c. (310) chocolate cookie crumbs
1/4 c. (60 ml) melted butter

FILLING:
1 1/2 lb. (3-250 g pkg.) cream cheese
3/4 c. (175 ml) sugar
3 eggs
1/4 c. (60 ml) raspberry glaze
5 oz. (142 g) bittersweet chocolate
fresh, whole raspberries to garnish
slivered almonds to garnish

- Pre-heat oven to 350 F.
- Combine crumbs and melted butter and press into the bottom of a nine-inch springform pan. Refrigerate.
- Soften the three packages of cream cheese, (you can microwave for 30 seconds) then beat with sugar until smooth.
- Add eggs, one at a time and mix until just blended.
- Stir in raspberry glaze (see recipe below) and the five squares of melted bittersweet baking chocolate.
- Pour into crust. Bake for 45 to 50 minutes or until the centre is almost set.
- Remove and run a knife around the edge to separate it from the pan, then cool completely on a rack.
- Refrigerate for three hours, or overnight.
- Carefully remove the side of the pan. Centre cheesecake on a serving plate.
- Before serving (several hours before is fine), pour raspberry glaze over top and allow it to drizzle down the sides.
- Decorate with fresh, whole raspberries and slivered almonds.
- Serves 12 or so.

FATHER'S DAY FEASTS

June is not only about the beginning of summer – it's also about dads.

When I was growing up, we would usually gather around the breakfast table to present our awkwardly-wrapped gifts to Dad. That way, he had all day to play with them.

You know, the pink caddis fly for fishing and the nifty neon barbecue apron; the cute organizer for his tools and the licence plate holder with the clever saying on it.

Or, perhaps in your family, it was a new fly rod, a high-tech barbecue, camouflage gear or a new dirt bike; a table saw or maybe even a Mustang.

We've done lots of things together on Dad's Day. We've spent time around a campfire up in the bush; in the boat on the lake; lounging on the deck; or watching a new video together.

Those charred hotdogs over a campfire or picnic lunches on the water were frequently a highlight of our day.

Maybe you've taken Dad bowling, or shopping, to a fancy restaurant, or out of the care home for the day. More than likely, at some point, he's gone to a baseball game.

Hopefully your Father's Day memories give everyone warm feelings to take away.

Whether the meals that day are created by the regular chef, or by the kids, they are a good excuse to get together and celebrate your feeling of family.

It seems my favourite men who are dads have all loved sweets, so desserts and cookies were always front and centre in that special day's feast.

Dad's Cookies

This was my Mom's recipe for Dad's Cookies and was probably her Mom's too. It could be a century old. The page is all covered in blotches and stains, and is grainy with dustings of flour. Sure, these are for dads, but little cookie monsters like them too. They certainly enjoy making them, even if they do have to save a few for Dad. (Dad really doesn't need many, anyway.)

1 c. (250 ml) flour
1 c. (250 ml) coconut
1 c. (250 ml) brown sugar
1 tsp. (5 ml) baking powder
1/2 tsp. (2 ml) baking soda
pinch of salt
1/2 c. (125 ml) butter
1 c. (250 ml) oatmeal
2 eggs
1 tsp. (5 ml) vanilla

- Thoroughly mix all dry ingredients except oatmeal. Rub in the butter using a pastry blender, fingers or a wooden spoon until the whole mixture is consistent.
- Work in the oatmeal.
- Beat eggs in a separate bowl and stir in the vanilla. Add that mixture to the dry ingredients.
- Drop by spoonful onto a greased baking sheet and pat down.
- Bake in 375-degree oven until just brown.

Em's Cookies

Em's not a precise cook and everything goes into these but the kitchen sink, yet her Dad has always loved them. Probably your Dad will too.

1/2 c. (125 ml) butter
1/2 c. (125 ml) white sugar
1/2 c. (125 ml) brown sugar
1 egg
1/2 tsp. (2 ml) vanilla
1/2 c. (125 ml) flour
1/2 c. (125 ml) whole wheat flour
1/2 tsp. (2 ml) baking soda
1/2 tsp. (2 ml) baking powder
1/2 tsp. (2 ml) salt
1 c. (250 ml) rolled oats
1/2 c. (125 ml) oat cereal rings
1/2 c. (125 ml) wheat squares cereal
1/2 c. (125 ml) crisp rice cereal
1/2 c. (125 ml) chocolate chips
1/2 c. (125 ml) peanut butter

- Pre-heat oven to 375 F.
- Cream butter with sugars, egg and vanilla.
- Stir in rest of ingredients. You may substitute or eliminate some of the cereals and grains. They do add a little nutrition and crunch to the cookies.
- Drop dough by teaspoon, two inches apart on an ungreased baking sheet.
- Bake 10 minutes or until brown.

See photograph on page **73**

Ginger Snaps

For some reason ginger snaps always make me think of Dads, too. This is one of the best recipes I've ever tried for these old favorites. I got it from Bernice and then discovered it was exactly the same recipe as my Mom's. I've also made these with a knob of grated fresh ginger instead of the dried, ground kind, and it raises them to a whole new level in flavour.

3/4 c. (175 ml) butter
1 c. (250 ml) brown sugar
1 egg
1/4 c. (60 ml) molasses
2 c. (500 ml) flour
1 tbsp. (15 ml) ground ginger
2 tsp. (10 ml) baking soda
1 tsp. (5 ml) cinnamon
1/2 tsp. (3 ml) cloves

- Pre-heat oven to 375 F.
- Cream butter (or butter) and sugar, and then beat in the egg and molasses.
- Whisk dry ingredients together and add to creamed mixture.
- Blend well, then form into small balls and roll in white sugar.
- Place two inches apart on an ungreased baking sheet.
- Bake for about eight minutes.
- They burn easily, so check the time required to brown the first batch.

Bacon & Chive Spud Salad

If you use low-fat sour cream, this is a lean alternative to the common potato salad and it's simply delicious. This is good picnic food. Fresh chives are at their absolute best in spring and early summer. Dads love potato salad.

5 medium red potatoes
2 bacon rashers
1/3 c. (75 ml) chives
1/2 c. (125 ml) sour cream
1/2 c. (125 ml) yogurt
salt and pepper to taste

- Wash but don't peel potatoes and simmer them until barely tender. Cut in half first if they're large.
- Drain thoroughly, then cut into half-inch cubes and let them cool.
- Meanwhile cook the bacon until crisp, drain well and chop finely.
- Combine the sour cream, yogurt and fresh, chopped chives, or green onions, salt and pepper. You may use low-fat sour cream and yogurt with excellent results.
- Toss gently with the cooled potato cubes until each one is coated, then sprinkle the bacon bits over the top.
- Serves 4-6.

WINE FOR GINGER SNAPS:
I would dunk these cookies in an Oh de Vie from Merridale Cidery, with a cup of coffee on the side. That is what Merridale calls the brandies it makes by distilling blackberries or apples.

Chocolate & Orange Ice Cream Pie

This is a family favourite. It's so rich a little slice goes a long way. At least that's what I tell the family when they want more.

WINE FOR CHOCOLATE-ORANGE ICE CREAM PIE:
This would be grand with a glass of CedarCreek's "M" – a fortified wine a lot like a fine Madeira – or the Liqueur Muscat from La Frenz; or D'oro, the remarkable walnut wine from Vista D'oro Farms & Winery.

1/3 c. (75 ml) butter
1 1/2 c. (375 ml) chocolate baking crumbs
4 c. (1 l) ice cream
4 squares semi-sweet chocolate
1/2 c. (125 ml) butter
1/4 c. (60 ml) sugar
1 tbsp. (15 ml) orange liqueur
1 tbsp. (15 ml) orange zest
2 eggs
curls of orange zest and chocolate

- Melt butter, mix with chocolate crumbs and press into a nine-inch pie pan. (About 35 chocolate wafers are required, if you can't find ready-made crumbs).
- Chill in the freezer for a few minutes and remove the ice cream and let it soften a bit.
- Scoop vanilla ice cream into the bottom of the pie shell, leaving a depression in the centre for the chocolate filling.
- Return to freezer.
- Melt baking chocolate (two minutes on medium in the microwave oven) and let cool while you assemble the other ingredients.
- Cream butter, then gradually add the sugar, beating until it's fluffy.
- Add melted chocolate and orange liqueur (or use orange flavouring) and chopped zest of a large orange. Beat in well.
- Add eggs, one at a time, beating for a couple of minutes after each addition, until the mixture thickens and is creamy.
- Spoon into the centre of the ice cream pie and freeze until set. (Allow a couple of hours at least.)
- Remove from the freezer about 15 minutes before serving. Rub the bottom and sides of the dish with a very hot, wet cloth to ensure it separates easily from the pie plate when you're serving.
- If there's any left, return it to the freezer.

Spinach Meatloaf Pinwheel

Most dads love meat and potatoes, but for a fancier version of that old standby, try this beef pinwheel, with steamed little new potatoes on the side. It's not difficult to make, and looks fabulous sliced and arranged on a platter, with the green spinach filling contrasting with the ground meat. It's also a real treat to eat.

Even lean ground meat is one of the cheaper meat buys, and spinach is also inexpensive.

You could also wrap the filling up in a solid piece of meat such as butterflied flank steak or rib eye roast.

FILLING:
10 oz. (300 g) frozen spinach
1 large onion
1 c. (250 ml) mushrooms
1 tbsp. (15 ml) butter
2 tbsp. (30 ml) fresh parsley
1/2 c. (125 ml) bread crumbs
1 egg
1/3 c. (75 ml) Swiss cheese, grated
1/2 tsp. (2 ml) salt
1/4 tsp. (1 ml) pepper
pinch of nutmeg

MEATLOAF:
1.5 lb. (700 g) ground beef
1/2 c. (125 ml) bread crumbs
1 tbsp. (15 ml) Worcestershire
1 egg
1 tsp. (5 ml) salt
1/4 tsp. (1 ml) pepper
fresh parsley, to garnish

- Prepare filling by thawing frozen spinach and squeezing out any excess moisture. Set aside.
- Chop onion and slice mushrooms. Melt butter or oil in a large frypan and cook over medium heat until onion is translucent and soft.
- Remove from heat and stir in chopped fresh parsley, fine dry bread crumbs, egg, grated cheese and seasonings.
- Allow to cool while you make up the meat mixture.
- Pre-heat oven to 350 F.
- Combine lean ground beef (you may substitute a small amount of lean ground pork for some of the beef for flavour), bread crumbs, Worcestershire sauce, egg, salt and freshly-ground pepper until thoroughly mixed. For the best results, conclude by using your hands.
- Spread a 20-inch long piece of wax paper on the counter. Pat the meat mixture onto it, creating an 18-inch by eight-inch rectangle.

CONTINUED ON PAGE 67

WINE FOR SPINACH MEATLOAF PINWHEEL:
A good-tasting budget meal calls for a good-tasting budget red, like the Merlot Cabernet blends from Calona Vineyards or Hester Creek.

CONTINUED FROM PAGE 66

- Finish by laying another sheet of wax paper over top and levelling it with a rolling pin or bottle, squaring the edges with your hands.
- Remove the top sheet of waxed paper and spread the filling evenly, leaving a half-inch border.
- Grease a 4x8-inch loaf pan, then carefully roll up the pinwheel, peeling off the bottom paper as you go. It should be eight inches wide.
- Lift it up and smoothly ease it into the pan.
- It may be cooked in a larger pan, but if it's a tight fit it will stay nice and round.
- This can be done ahead of time and refrigerated for a few hours.
- Bake for about an hour.
- Remove from pan and slice thickly. Arrange on a serving board or platter so the pinwheel pattern is evident. Garnish with fresh parsley.
- Serves 6.

See photograph on page **73**

6. Patio Parties

CELEBRATE CANADA

Certain occasions simply demand a party, and in the summer, it usually takes place outdoors.

With a variety of local farm-fresh fruits and vegetables now ripe and ready, include them in your plans, along with the freshest meat and fish you can find.

To make it fun for you as well as your guests, reduce the cleanup by making use of some of the pretty disposable tableware available now.

I draw the line at plastic cutlery, since it's next to useless for anything but stirring a drink, but you could pick up some odds and ends of cutlery at a second hand store for use on the patio.

If you're concerned that paper plates aren't solid enough, support them with wicker plates underneath, and there will still be no dishes to do.

Even better, use food as containers. Try buns, pita breads, wraps, crackers, potato skins or other edible containers for your meat and vegetables. That way, there's minimum cleanup because everyone eats their own dishes.

Finger food is fun, but fancy too. Instead of a sit-down meal requiring a full place setting, have a stand-up-and-move-around meal.

If it's to be a casual affair, offer your guests the option of contributing food. It's interesting to see what tasty specialties people bring to show off, and it reduces the work for you.

If it's not a Canada Day or birthday party, plan something flashy, by establishing a theme for the event, whether colors, countries of origin, a favourite movie, or an era in time, and ask that all the food and dress fit that theme.

Whatever you choose, prepare as much ahead of time as possible then you can sit back and relax with your friends or family when the party starts.

Em's Crab & Artichoke Dip

This has a delicate flavour with just a bit of a bite and makes a great dip for pita crisps, corn or tortilla chips, or chunks of French bread. You can make it thicker or thinner by varying the quantity of cream used.

WINE FOR EM'S CRAB AND ARTICHOKE DIP:
I'd like a glass or two of Kerner from Oliver Twist, Gray Monk or Summer Gate wineries. What better wine for a party than a fragrant white from a grape developed in Germany and named for a man who was minor poet, a doctor, a painter and a coffin maker – a great conversation piece.

4 green onions
2 cloves garlic
6 oz (170 g) artichoke hearts
4 oz. (120 g) crabmeat
2 c. (500 ml) fresh spinach
2 tbsp. (30 ml) sweet red pepper
2 tbsp. (15 ml) olive oil
1/4 c. (60 ml) heavy cream
1/4 tsp. (1 ml) hot pepper flakes
1/2 c. (125 ml) cream cheese
fresh parsley or other herbs, to garnish

- Pre-heat oven to 375 F.
- Chop green onions and mince garlic. Chop up artichoke hearts. Rinse crab and drain well. Chop spinach and mince peppers.
- Heat a non-stick pan to medium-high, add olive oil and onions cooking for a few minutes before adding the garlic and stirring until soft.
- Add the artichoke hearts and crab, then spinach, cream, red pepper, dried hot peppers and cream cheese.
- Stir and let everything simmer for a few minutes.
- Spoon into a larger ovenproof serving dish or smaller individual ones and bake for 7 to 10 minutes.
- Serves 4 or so.

Guacamole

Everyone loves the silky texture and rich taste of Mexican Guacamole, served as a dip for tortilla chips or pita crisps.

2 avocadoes
1 small tomato
1/4 mild, sweet onion
1 tbsp. (15 ml) mayonnaise
2 tsp. (10 ml) Worcestershire
6 drops hot sauce
salt to taste

- Choose firm but ripe avocadoes. Halve and remove the seed. Remove the flesh with a spoon and mash it up in a medium-sized bowl.
- Mince a small tomato and about a quarter of a mild red or bermuda-type sweet onion. Add to the mashed avocado, along with the mayonnaise, Worcestershire sauce and hot sauce.
- Gently mix together without mushing the tomato.

Taste before adding salt, as the chips are often fairly salty.

Serves 3-4.

Prawn & Spinach Tartlettes

This great filling is easy to make and it looks scrumptious in these easy wonton wrapper tart shells. They make any occasion extra special. Serve hot or cold.

24 wonton wrappers
2 green onions
4 c. (1 l) fresh spinach
6 tbsp. (90 ml) cream cheese
2 tbsp. (30 ml) parmesan cheese
12 prawns
2 tsp. (10 ml) dry white wine
salt and pepper, to taste
parmesan to garnish

- Pre-heat oven to 375 F.
- Carefully separate square wonton wrappers and gently press them into 24 mini muffin cups.
- Mince green onion and wash and chop spinach.
- Wilt spinach by microwaving for about 2 minutes.
- Combine cream cheese, parmesan and minced green onions in a large glass bowl and microwave for 45 seconds to one minute.
- Stir, then add spinach and combine thoroughly. Taste and season.
- Cut prawns in half and poach in the white wine for one to two minutes in the microwave, or on the stove, cooking just until they start to turn pink. Drain wine into spinach mixture and stir in.
- Spoon spinach into wonton wrap-per shells, dividing it among the 24. Top with poached prawn pieces and sprinkle each with a bit of parmesan cheese.
- Bake in a hot oven for seven to 10 minutes until the shell has browned a bit.
- Makes 24.

See photograph on page **74**

Humus

Legumes such as chick peas, which (also known as garbanzo beans), are great substitutes for meats in a vegetarian diet, or for those wanting to lower their cholesterol. Fresh, torn pita breads are great used to scoop up this Greek-inspired dip.

19 oz. (540 ml) tin of chick peas
2 cloves garlic
2 tsp. (10 ml) lemon juice
1 tbsp. (15 ml) olive oil
1 tsp. (5 ml) sesame oil
salt, to taste
fresh, chopped parsley

- Drain and mash the chick peas in a bowl, and add crushed, minced garlic, fresh lemon juice and oils.
- Mix thoroughly and add salt if needed. Garnish with chopped parsley.

WINE FOR PRAWN & SPINACH TARTLETTES:
I recommend a Pinot Gris, a wine with the flavours and the acidity that will lift all of the wonderful tastes in this dish.

Herb & Spinach Bites

These are great to make ahead as a cold snack or appetizer or as part of a stand-up main meal on the patio.

6 eggs
3 tbsp. (45 ml) cream
2 tbsp. (45 ml) fresh parsley
1 tbsp. (15 ml) fresh tarragon
1 tsp. (5 ml) fresh thyme
1/4 tsp. (1 ml) salt
1/2 tsp. (2 ml) pepper
1/3 c. (75 ml) parmesan
1/2 lb. (225 g) mushrooms
6 green onions
1 10-oz. (300-g) pkg. frozen spinach
butter
1/2 c. (125 ml) Swiss cheese

WINE FOR HERB AND SPINACH BITES:
With this, I would like the zesty flavours of Sauvignon Blanc and blends based on that variety. My favourites include Little Straw, Gehringer Brothers and Jackson-Triggs Sauvignon Blanc or the Graves styling of Clos du Soleil's Capella.

- Pre-heat oven to 375 F.
- Beat eggs with cream, fresh, minced herbs, spices and grated parmesan cheese, in a large bowl. Set aside.
- Slice mushrooms and green onions and saute in a non-stick pan in just a smidge of melted butter for a few minutes until they're soft.
- The amount of spinach isn't critical, and it can be either fresh or frozen. If fresh, chop and barely wilt, either in the microwave oven or in the frypan with the mushrooms. (You'll have to use a much larger pan than you would otherwise. If frozen, thaw and squeeze out as much of the water as possible.)
- Add green onions, mushrooms, spinach and half the grated cheese (cheddar would be okay too), to the egg mixture and combine well.
- Pour into a two-quart casserole, quiche dish or a square cake pan that has been greased lightly.
- Sprinkle the remaining cheese on top and bake for 20-25 minutes.
- Cool slightly and cut into squares. The size you cut them into depends on how you intend to use them.

See photograph on page **74**

Chili

What's a patio party without the chili? I think this is a particularly excellent one, and others have said it's just right too. It has evolved over the years. Spice it up to your own taste. This makes a medium-spicy one. Double the recipe to serve more people.

2 cloves garlic
1 large onion
1 lb. (454 g) lean ground beef
3-4 c. (750 ml) tomato sauce
14 oz. (400 ml) kidney beans
2-3 tbsp. (30-45 ml) chili powder
2 tbsp. (30 ml) fresh oregano
1 tbsp. (15 ml) fresh basil
1 tsp. (5 ml) brown sugar
1/4 tsp. (1 ml) cayenne pepper
8 small mushrooms
salt and pepper, to taste

- Chop onion and mince garlic and herbs.
- Soften chopped onions with garlic in a drizzle of oil on medium heat in a large pot or Dutch oven, then add the ground beef. Stir regularly until it loses its pinkness, then add tomato sauce, kidney beans, herbs and spices.
- Add more or less chili powder and cayenne pepper so it turns out as hot or as mild as you'd like. Bring back to a bubble, stirring, and add whole small mushrooms.
- Turn down the heat and simmer, covered, for an hour or two, or pour into a slow cooker and leave on the low setting for four to six hours.
- Taste for seasoning, adjust, and serve with warm rolls or fresh bread, and perhaps a salad on the side.
- Makes 4 to 6 servings.

WINE FOR CHILI:
The more robust the red, the better. Robin's Return from Robin's Ridge, Salt Spring Vineyard's Millotage, Stoneboat's Pinotage, Larch Hills's Grandview Bench Red.

TOP:
**Em's
Cookies**

Recipe on
page **63**

BOTTOM:
**Spinach
Meatloaf
Pinwheel**

Recipe on
page **66**

TOP:
Prawn & Spinach Tartlettes

Recipe on
page **70**

BOTTOM:
Herb & Spinach Bites

Recipe on
page **71**

TOP:
Cherry Chocolate Cheesecake

Recipe on page **79**

BOTTOM:
Cherry Clafoutis

Recipe on page **80**

TOP:
Blueberry Frozen Yogurt
Recipe on page **81**

BOTTOM::
Beef & Herb-stuffed Zucchini
Recipe on page **86**

Watermelon Basket of Fruit

This makes a dramatic table centre-piece as well as a refreshing dessert for a patio party or any summer occasion.

1 watermelon
1 honeydew melon
2 kiwis
1 c. (250 ml) blueberries
1/2 c. (125 ml) grapes
1 c. (250 ml) strawberries
1 c. (250 ml) mandarin orange pieces
1/4 c. (60 ml) orange liqueur

WINE FOR WATERMELON BASKET OF FRUIT: *This would be great with a pink sparkling wine like Gray Monk's Rosé Brut or Summerhill's Cipes Ice, which has a bit of Icewine to sweeten the taste.*

- Begin by carving the watermelon, much as you would a pumpkin at Halloween. Choose the flattest part of the watermelon as the base for your basket so it doesn't roll over when it's full of fruit salad.
- Use a marker to draw a handle over the top of the watermelon, then draw approximately where the top of the basket will be between the handle.
- Remove two wedges on either side, leaving the handle intact, then begin to remove large chunks of pulp. Form into balls with a melon baller. (Cubes are fine, too.)
- When you've removed most of the red flesh, scallop or cut teeth along the top edge of the basket before you begin to fill it with fruit.
- Cut the watermelon and honeydew into small cubes or balls.
- Peel and slice kiwis thickly, halving or quartering each slice.
- Use fresh or frozen blueberries, and seedless grapes, either red or green.
- Hull strawberries and section oranges, or use tinned mandarins. Substitute fresh apricots or plums for the oranges, if you prefer.
- Gently and carefully lift the fruit to mix it without mushing or breaking it up, then pour liqueur over it. You may substitute a juice of your choice.
- Carefully lift and turn again to distribute it.
- Refrigerate for a few hours until it's time to serve it.
- Garnish the top with fresh mint leaves or edible flowers.

Mom's Fruit Surprise

This is literally a surprise every time you make it because it depends on the fruit that's in season. Think about the colors you want to combine before deciding on which fruit you will include, and which flavor and color of jelly powder you'd like.

2 c. (500 ml) berries
6 fresh peaches
1 c. (250 ml) red or green grapes
19 oz. (540 ml) pineapple
10 oz. (284 ml) Mandarin oranges
1/2 c. (125 ml) cherries
1 pkg. jello
1 tbsp. (15 ml) lemon juice

- For the berries, combine strawberries, raspberries, blueberries or blackberries either fresh or frozen, but unsweetened.
- Nectarines or apricots may be substituted for the peaches, or canned, drained, unsweetened peaches for fresh.
- Choose seedless grapes and pit fresh cherries, or substitute maraschino or canned ones, drained.
- Drain a can of pineapple tidbits and another of Mandarin orange segments.
- Pit cherries.
- Sliced bananas and peeled, cut-up kiwi fruit or pears are other possible fruits to use.

- Make up the jelly, minus one cup of the liquid called for in the package directions. Cool it until it begins to jell and has the consistency of honey.
- This takes a couple of hours in the refrigerator.
- Wash out a large serving bowl with cold water, and add the fruits, jello and lemon juice, mixing together well.
- Top with whipped cream when serving, if desired.
- Serves 8-10.

Cherry Chocolate Cheesecake

This small cheesecake is so sweet and rich-tasting that a thin slice goes a long way, so you can provide dessert for at least 16 people with an 8-inch cake. It's like candy. More than one box of chocolate squares is needed to make both the cake and its chocolate outer shell.

The cake can be made the day ahead and refrigerated; then the topping added on the day you're serving it.

BASE:

1 c. (250 ml) chocolate crumbs
3 tbsp. (45 ml) melted butter

FILLING:

1 lb. (500 g) cream cheese, softened
1 c. (250 ml) sugar
3 eggs
1/2 c. (125 ml) cherry juice concentrate
6 oz. (175 g) bittersweet chocolate, melted
1/2 c. (125 ml) sour cream

TOPPING:

4 oz. (125 g) bittersweet chocolate
2 tbsp. (30 ml) butter
1/2 c. (125 ml) sifted icing sugar
2 tbsp. (30 ml) cherry juice concentrate

fresh cherry halves, to garnish

- For the crust, combine the melted butter with the crumbs and press into the bottom of an eight-inch springform pan. Refrigerate while you make the filling.

- Pre-heat oven to 350 F.
- Beat softened blocks (you could microwave them for 30 seconds) of cream cheese with an electric beater and add the sugar.
- Adding one egg at a time, beat on low speed to combine.
- Add cherry juice concentrate, a cherry-flavoured brandy or cherry flavouring, then melt chocolate and add, blending in until the mixture is smooth. Add sour cream.
- Spread over the crust, sit the pan on a cookie sheet and bake for an hour, or just until the centre is set.
- Remove and immediatly run a knife around the edge of the pan to release the edge from the pan. Let cool for about 10 minutes before removing the side of the pan. Once it's cooled, refrigerate until ready to enclose in its chocolate shell. This can be done a day ahead.
- For the topping, melt the chocolate and stir in the butter until it's melted. Sift, then add icing sugar, mixing in well. Then add enough cherry concentrate or flavouring to make it the right consistency to spread over the cheesecake. It won't be a thick layer, so leave enough for the sides.
- Return it to the refrigerator to set the topping.
- At the last minute, decorate with pitted fresh cherries, cut in half, all around the edges, and perhaps a light dusting of icing sugar.

See photograph on page **75**

WINE FOR CHERRY CHOCOLATE CHEESECAKE:
The chocolate and cherry flavours need a glass of blackberry port such as Cherry Point's Solera, Averill Creek's Cowichan Black or Beaufort Vineyards's Black

Cherry Clafoutis

This looks delicious and the eggy batter provides a lovely nest for the cherries, or other fruit such as plums or apricots. Outside of cherry season, you can use frozen or canned fruit, but thoroughly drain it first. Clafoutis is a traditional French dessert, but each cook makes personal variations. For a different presentation, use individual custard cups instead of a casserole dish.

1 lb. (454 g) cherries
1 tbsp. (15 ml) brandy or sherry
1/2 c. (125 ml) sugar
1/2 c. (125 ml) flour
pinch of salt
1 1/4 c. (310 ml) milk
3 eggs

- Heat oven to 425 F.
- Pit cherries into the bottom of a greased (I use a spray oil) glass casserole dish or deep pie pan.
- Drizzle them with a little brandy or dry sherry.
- In a bowl, combine all the remaining ingredients. Whisk until smooth. Pour over the fruit.
- Put into a hot oven and immediately turn it down to 375 F.
- Bake until it has risen and browned lightly, about 30 minutes or so.
- Sprinkle with icing sugar if you like, before serving.
- This can be served at room temperature, but be prepared for it to fall once it's removed from the oven.
- Serves 8.

See photograph on page **75**

Blueberry Lemon Cake

This is full of fresh lemon flavour, and it needs no icing so it packs neatly into a picnic hamper or lunch bag.

2 c. (500 ml) blueberries
2 lemons
4 eggs
1 3/4 c. (420 ml) sugar
1 c. (250 ml) oil
2 tsp. (10 ml) vanilla
2 1/2 c. (600 ml) flour
2 tsp. (10 ml) baking powder

- Pre-heat oven to 350 F and grease a 10-inch bundt or tube pan.
- Sprinkle half cup or so of blueberries over the bottom of the bundt pan.
- Using a zester or grater, remove only the yellow part of the rind of both lemons, and chop it up finely.
- Separate eggs, putting whites into a large mixing bowl and yolks into a small one. Beat the whites until they are frothy and beginning to thicken.
- Beat egg yolks and add sugar, oil, vanilla, juice from both lemons, and minced zest.
- Whisk flour and baking powder together.
- Fold dry ingredients into egg mixture, then blueberries. If using frozen ones, sprinkle a bit of flour in to separate them. Use them while frozen.
- Pour batter over blueberries into tube pan and bake in 350 F oven for one hour.
- When cool, turn out onto a cake plate and serve.

Bernice's Blueberry Buckle

No, I don't know where the name came from. Isn't it delightful? It's also a delicious dessert, especially with fresh blueberries and a dollop of whipped cream. But, you could also substitute peaches for half or all the blueberries for a yummy twist.

1/4 c. (60 ml) margarine
1/2 c. (125 ml) white sugar
1 egg
1 c. (250 ml) flour
1 1/2 tsp. (8 ml) baking powder
1/4 tsp. (1 ml) salt
1/3 c. (75 ml) milk
2 c. (500 ml) blueberries

TOPPING:
1/3 c. (75 ml) sugar
1/4 c. (60 ml) margarine
1/3 c. (75 ml) flour
1 tsp. (5 ml) cinnamon

- Pre-heat oven to 350 degrees F.
- Cream margarine and sugar. Beat in egg. Whisk together dry ingredients in a separate bowl, then add to egg mixture. Add milk and blend.
- Spread in greased 8x8-inch pan.
- Spread blueberries (fresh or frozen) on top.
- Mix topping ingredients together until crumbly. Scatter over blueberries.
- Bake for 40-50 min.
- Serves 9.

WINE FOR BLUEBERRY FROZEN YOGURT:
I differ from the conventional wisdom of serving Icewine with sweet desserts because the Icewine, whose flavours are more delicate than is appreciated, often gets swamped. I prefer a glass of mistelle, or fortified fruit wine. Forbidden Fruit offers Plumiscuous, a fortified red plum wine, and Caught, a fortified apricot wine.

Blueberry Frozen Yogurt

This can be doubled to fill the ice cream maker, and it's just bursting with flavour, but not calories. You could use fresh, Fraser Valley blueberries, or substitute strawberries, raspberries or cherries from the Okanagan.

1 c. (250 ml) blueberries
1 c. (250 ml) low-fat plain yogurt
2 tbsp. (30 ml) sugar

- Puree berries in a blender, then add yogurt and a bit of sugar, if you like.
- Pour into the frozen bowl of your ice cream maker and follow the equipment's instructions.
- If there's any left once it's been freshly made, it does get quite hard put in the freezer, so you'll have to remove it to sit for a few minutes before serving.

See photograph on page **76**

7. Heavenly Herbs

GROWN IN B.C.

By mid-summer we can expect company, because everyone knows B.C. is a great place for a holiday.

That means you'll be cooking for more rumbling tummies than usual, so simplicity is the order of the day. Uncomplicated recipes and fresh, local ingredients create the best cuisine there is.

B.C. Day, the first Monday in August, should remind us to include B.C. fresh products in our meal plans, including fish and seafood, fruit and vegetables, pork, beef, chicken and lamb, as well as eggs and dairy products such as cheeses and yogurt.

From the fruits of the sea along our coast to the green and verdant fields of the Fraser Valley, to the lush orchards and vineyards of the Okanagan, the range lands of the Cariboo and the fields of grain in the Peace, we're constantly reminded of our farming heritage, and summer is the time of year we can celebrate that essential part of our culture and heritage.

B.C. has the most diverse agricultural area in Canada, and our world-class chefs take good advantage of it. We should take a page from their book.

This is the time of year when we harvest the widest variety of fresh fruits, either to eat fresh or to preserve for reminders of summer when the snow begins to drift down.

There are fresh cherries, strawberries, blueberries and raspberries, apricots, nectarines and peaches, plums, grapes, summer apples and pears.

Try mixing together some of your favourite fruits which have been pitted, peeled and chopped, if necessary, into a kind of fresh fruit salsa, to accompany your favourite fish, pork or chicken, hot from the barbecue, pan or oven.

Add a few chopped fresh herbs such as cilantro, mint or parsley, a drizzle of honey and a sprinkle of powdered cumin, cayenne pepper or lime juice, and you'll have created a fresh-tasting, unusual accompaniment which will elevate a simple meal to a divine one.

Those who love to cook invariably have a healthy appreciation for the complex flavors fresh herbs contribute to their creations.

Remember that we can use less salt when foods are seasoned liberally with herbs.

There's nothing quite as fine as using your own fresh herbs to season meals now, and using your own dried ones next winter. Bottles of dried herbs or herb vinegars make wonderful Christmas gifts too.

Tabbouleh Salad

This Middle Eastern salad is not only deliciously different, but nutritious, too, since it uses the whole wheat grain and contains lots of fresh vegetables. It's terrific to take along on a picnic.

WINE FOR
TABBOULEH
SALAD:
*Can there be a
picnic without
rosé? Take along a
bottle of
Rigamarole Rosé or
Tamarack Rosé
from Larch Hills.
Another choice for
that picnic basket
is Mad Angie, as
Larch Hills calls its
Madeleine
Angevine white.*

1 c. (250 ml) bulgur
2 tomatoes
1 sweet onion
1 green pepper
1/2 c. (125 ml) fresh parsley
2 tbsp. (30 ml) fresh mint
1/4 c. (60 ml) lemon juice
1 tsp. (5 ml) salt
freshly-ground pepper
1/4 c. (60 ml) olive oil

- Soak the bulgur (crushed wheat) in ample cold water for half an hour or so. Drain well, then squeeze dry.
- Chop tomatoes, a mild, sweet onion, (green onion could be substituted), green pepper (optional), fresh parsley and mint.
- Toss gently together with bulgur.
- Add lemon juice, salt and fresh-ground black pepper.
- Add the olive oil at the last minute and mix gently, but thoroughly.
- Garnish with fresh sprigs of parsley or mint.
- This could be served on a large lettuce leaf or scooped up with chunks of fresh pita bread.
- Serves 4-6.

New Nugget Potatoes

A sprinkle of curry powder or a sprinkling of chives or cilantro brings baby nugget potatoes to life, but so does a handful of dill. Use whatever number of potatoes you feel are needed for the crowd, and adjust the other ingredients accordingly.

6-8 little new potatoes
1 small onion
2 tsp. (10 ml) butter
1 tsp. (5 ml) curry powder
fresh cilantro, to garnish

- Steam small potatoes over medium-low heat until just cooked, but remove them before they begin to come apart.
- Finely chop a small onion.
- Melt butter in a small non-stick pan and add the chopped onion, cooking over moderate heat for a few minutes until soft.
- Add a prepared curry mixture or garam masala, stirring into the butter and onion and cooking for a minute or so.
- Roll the potatoes in this mixture, until they're nicely coated.
- Garnish with a bit of chopped cilantro.
- Or, mince a couple of green onions and a fist full of fresh dill and toss it all into the drained, hot potatoes with a pat of butter. Mix well to coat the potatoes.

Herbed Carrots

This varies with whatever herbs are fresh, and whether you have little fresh carrots out of the garden, or larger produce section vegetables. Incidentally, this even revives aging carrots.

4-6 carrots
1 tbsp. (15 ml) butter
3 green onions
1 tbsp. (15 ml) parsley
1 tsp. (5 ml) oregano
1/2 tsp. (2 ml) thyme
1/2 tsp. (2 ml) brown sugar
1 tbsp. (15 ml) white wine
2 tbsp. (30 ml) water
salt and pepper to taste

- Scrub carrots and cut into 2-inch pieces. If they're thick, cut in half lengthwise.
- Melt butter in a hot frypan with a tight lid. Add carrots and stir them in the butter until they begin to brown. Add chopped green onions, minced herbs, sugar and wine. Then add the water. Cover tightly, bring to bubbling and reduce heat to low for 15 to 20 minutes until there's very little liquid left and the carrots are tender.
- Sprinkle with fresh chopped parsley before serving.
- Serves four.

Mint Sauce

The English particularly like mint sauce or mint jelly with lamb, while the Greeks prefer garlic, lemon, oregano and thyme with theirs.

3 tbsp. (45 ml) water
2 tbsp. (30 ml) sugar
1/2 c. (125 ml) vinegar
1/2 c. (125 ml) mint leaves

- Harvest the mint early in the morning and remove the leaves. Chop them finely.
- Make a syrup by heating the water and dissolving the sugar in it.
- Cool and add the mint leaves and a good, flavourful vinegar.
- Keep refrigerated.

WINE FOR MINT SAUCE:
None. Mint and ginger are two flavours that are ill-starred with most wines.

Trout with Green Onions & Mushrooms

The mild flavours of green onions and mushrooms complement the delicate flavour of fresh trout. Boiled potatoes and a mild-flavoured green vegetable such as asparagus or fresh beans are delicious with this. You may substitute a fresh kokanee and try fresh dill instead of – or with – the fresh parsley and chives.

WINE FOR TROUT WITH GREEN ONIONS & MUSHROOMS: *This calls for a good crisp Riesling from Tantalus or Sperling or Quails' Gate or a Chenin Blanc from Road 13 or Quails' Gate.*

2 trout
4 green onions
8 mushrooms
drizzle of oil
dab of butter
flour, cornmeal, salt and pepper
1 lemon
fresh parsley or chives to garnish
lemon slices

- Clean trout, or rinse if already cleaned, and remove head if desired.
- Trim and slice green onions and mushrooms.
- Heat cooking oil over medium-high heat in a non-stick frypan or a well-seasoned cast iron pan. Melt butter, swirl it around and immediately add green onions and mushrooms.
- Saute until cooked and brown, remove with a slotted spoon and keep warm.
- Meanwhile, dredge whole fish in a mixture of flour, cornmeal, salt and pepper to taste.
- Thinly slice a lemon and insert the slices into each fish.
- Immediately add fish to heated butter and oil mixture remaining in pan, first adding more fat if needed.
- Brown over medium-high heat until the flesh of the thickest part of the fish is just opaque, turning carefully just once.
- Don't overcook.
- Carefully remove to a serving platter, scraping brown bits from the pan over the fish and scattering the cooked onions and mushrooms over top.
- Garnish with chopped chives or parsley and remaining slices of lemon.
- Serves 2 to 4.

Beef & Herb-stuffed Zucchini

This looks quite dramatic so it's great for company. You can use any size of zucchini, but I think this is a good recipe for those ones that got away on you from the garden. There's not much room for stuffing the little guys and we treat this as a complete meal.

1 foot-long zucchini
1/2 lb. (227 g) lean ground beef
1 small onion
1 clove garlic
1 tbsp. (15 ml) chives
1 tbsp. (15 ml) parsley
2 tsp. (10 ml) lemon balm
1 tsp. (5 ml) fresh oregano
1 tsp. (5 ml) fresh tarragon
salt and pepper to taste
3 tbsp. (45 ml) white wine
grated Swiss cheese

- Pre-heat oven to 350 F.
- Cut zucchini in half lengthwise to form two long 'boats.' Use a spoon to remove the pulp from the centre of the vegetable, making sure you don't pierce the outer skin. Leave a shell of at least a half-inch all around.
- Chop the pulp, onions and mince the garlic.
- Use whatever herbs you have fresh that sound as if they'd be good. It's important there be a total of at least three tablespoons of fresh herbs, though. Mince them.
- Gently heat a drizzle of olive oil in a large frypan or wok and add the ground beef and onions, then the garlic.
- Cook until the beef has changed colour and the onions are limp, adding the chopped zucchini pulp part way through.
- When the pulp has cooked down and there's little juice left in the pan, add the herbs and wine and continue stirring and cooking until there's just enough moisture left for the stuffing to stick together.
- Salt and pepper each shell and stuff with the meat mixture. Grate Swiss cheese, or a combination of Swiss and mozzarella over the top and place the zucchini 'boats' in a pan with about a half-inch of water in the bottom.
- Roast for about half an hour, until the cheese has browned on top.
- Serve on a platter or serving board.
- For a vegetarian version, omit the meat and substitute any other vegetables you'd like, including lentils or black beans, more onion, chopped celery or tomato, and combine it with cooked rice before stuffing.
- For a richer version, add a thick bechamel (white) sauce to the top of the meat stuffing before the grated cheese.
- Serves 2-4.

See photograph on page **76**

WINE FOR BEEF & HERB-STUFFED ZUCCHINI:
I would like this with Mt. Boucherie's Gamay Noir, Sandhill's Sangiovese or Larch Hills's Lemberger.

Vegetable Layers with Basil & Cheese

This dish has wide appeal, even for those who profess not to care much for some of the individual components. The vegetables used can be varied according to what's available. For instance, asparagus, other summer squashes and eggplant are all good in this as well.

2 cloves garlic
1/4 c. (60 ml) olive oil
2 large potatoes
1 large onion
2 zucchini
2 tomatoes
1 1/2 c. (375 ml) swiss cheese
1 tbsp. (15 ml) fresh herbs
handful of fresh basil
salt and pepper, to taste

- Pre-heat oven to 425 F.
- Use a fairly shallow casserole dish, about 9x12 inches. Smush and peel the garlic cloves and heat the garlic in the olive oil in the casserole dish, turning it so the oil covers the bottom of the dish.
- Pour the garlic and remaining oil into a small bowl for use later.
- Thinly slice the potatoes, onion, zucchini and tomatoes and grate cheese.
- Arrange a layer of half of each vegetable, in that order, and sprinkle with salt and pepper, herbs of your choice (parsley, oregano, thyme and even a little tarragon are all good), and some of the grated cheese.
- Repeat with the remaining vegetables, topping it all with the remaining cheese. Pour the reserved garlic and olive oil evenly over the top.
- Cook, uncovered, in a pre-heated oven for 40-50 minutes, or until the vegetables are tender when pierced with a skewer.
- Pile the basil leaves and then roll them up from the side and slice them thinly.
- Remove the vegetables from the oven and sprinkle the shredded fresh basil over the top.
- Serves 4-6.

WINE FOR VEGETABLE LAYERS WITH BASIL & CHEESE: *This calls for a fruity white, like Sperling's Market White, Wild Goose's Autumn Gold, Little Straw's Tapestry or the Bacchus from either Domaine de Chaberton or Arrowleaf. A really exotic pairing would be Calona's Sovereign Opal, a perfumed wine unique to the Okanagan.*

Basil Pesto

I make up this recipe when the basil's ripe, omitting the parmesan cheese, then spoon dabs of it on a baking sheet and freeze them. Once they're hard, I pop them into a plastic freezer bag for individual use during the winter, when fresh basil and summer are distant memories.

Just add parmesan along with the frozen dab of pesto to your noodles or whatever.

2 c. (500 ml) packed fresh basil leaves
1/4 c. (60 ml) olive oil
1/4 c. (60 ml) toasted pine nuts
2 garlic cloves
pinch of salt
1/2 c. (125 ml) grated parmesan

- Toss everything but the parmesan cheese into the blender or food processor and blend on high until it forms a paste.
- Scrape out into a bowl and stir in the cheese.
- This can be served on hot cooked pasta such as fettucine, on pizza, on a broiled beef or salmon steak, on french bread as part of a bruschetta or just wherever fresh basil would be good if you had any on hand.

Tzatziki: Greek Yogurt Dip

This is a refreshing accompaniment to grilled meats such as lamb or chicken or it can be served as a dip for fresh vegetables or pita triangles. It's also an essential ingredient in a pita stuffed with Greek souvlaki or meat-balls – a delightful, light summer meal.

1 cucumber
1/2 c. (125 ml) green onions
1 garlic clove
2 c. (500 ml) plain yogurt

- Grate a large English cucumber, or a peeled garden cuke, then press to drain off most of the accumulated juice.
- Finely chop green onions and garlic clove.
- Add yogurt (skim yogurt is fine, but the richer you use, the richer the resulting dip will be). Gently but thoroughly mix in onions and garlic.
- This is better if it's made ahead and left to sit in the refrigerator during the day or overnight.
- Serves 2-6, depending on whether it's served as an appetizer or as a snack.

See photograph on page **93**

Smashed Meatballs in Pitas

We first tried something like these spicy, herb-infused meatballs many years ago in a Greek restaurant, stuffed into a pita bread with delicate, refreshing Tzatziki (yogurt and cucumber dip), chopped tomatoes, peppers and sweet onions. It was served in a special wooden holder, so it stood up instead of spilling out onto the table.

Because it's fist food, it's great to take camping. No dishes.

1 sweet onion
1 clove garlic
2 slices bread
2 tbsp. (30 ml) white wine
1 egg
1 lb. (454 g) lean ground beef
1 tbsp. (15 ml) fresh mint
1 tbsp. (15 ml) fresh parsley
1 tsp. (5 ml) fresh oregano
1 tbsp. (15 ml) tomato sauce
salt and pepper to taste

WINE FOR SMASHED MEATBALLS IN PITAS: *This calls for a red that is approachable and affordable, like Mission Hill's Five Vineyards Cabernet Merlot or Prospect Winery's Shiraz or Rollingdale's Tumbleweed Red.*

- Cook chopped onion and minced garlic until softened, then place in a large bowl.
- Tear bread into small pieces and soak in the white wine, then toss into the bowl with the onion.
- Mince fresh herbs.
- Add beaten egg, ground beef, minced herbs, spices and tomato sauce and stir together thoroughly until it's fluffy, using a wooden spoon or your hands.
- Form into small balls, about an inch in diameter, arrange on a cookie sheet, then squash flat.
- Bake in a 350 F oven for about 20 minutes.
- These are delicious served as an appetizer; with a spicy tomato sauce prior to the main course; or in halved, opened pita breads with a yogurt and cucumber tzatziki, bits of tomato, onion and green pepper, as a light meal.
- Serves 4-6.

See photograph on page **93**

Winnie's Apricot Scones

These have sweet/tart surprise bites throughout, and can be served for breakfast, brunch, as a snack, or in lunches. Great to take camping.

2 c. (500 ml) flour
1/4 c. (60 ml) sugar
1 1/2 tsp. (2 ml) baking powder
1/4 c. (60 ml) cold butter
1/2 c. (125 ml) milk
1/2 c. (125 ml) plain yogurt
1 egg
1 tsp. (5 ml) lemon zest
pinch of salt
1 c. (250 ml) fresh apricots

- Pre-heat oven to 375 F.
- Combine flour, sugar and baking powder in a large bowl. Cut in butter until it resembles coarse crumbs.
- Make a well in the centre.
- In a small bowl, whisk together the milk, yogurt, egg and minced lemon zest.
- Pour into the well and bring together with a fork, just until combined.
- Gently incorporate chopped, pitted, fresh apricots.
- Drop by spoonful onto a baking sheet, greased or lined with a silicone baking mat or parchment paper.
- Bake for about 25 minutes or until golden brown.
- Makes about 15, depending on the size.

Ginger Peach Salsa

Peaches picked ripe and fresh off the tree are a true flavour treat. This is good alongside ham or grilled chicken or pork.

3 peaches
1 tbsp. (15 ml) ginger
1 tbsp. (15 ml) brown sugar
1 tbsp. (15 ml) lemon juice
1/2 tsp. (2 ml) lemon zest

- Peel and very finely chop peaches. Canned ones can be used.
- Mince fresh ginger and combine with peaches.
- Add sugar, lemon juice and minced lemon zest.
- Heat just before using, either in the microwave or on the barbecue, and serve over or with barbecued meat.
- Serves 4-6.

See photograph on page 93

8. Harvest the Bounty

GAD ZUKES

Harvest time is just about the most exciting time of year for anyone who loves food. And, in this part of the world, late summer is when the widest variety of fruits and vegetables are available fresh. It's enough to overwhelm the senses. And, when the zucchini are ripe, it's enough to overwhelm the kitchen.

But the pulses quicken for most people when September nears and the routine of autumn gets underway again.

That can mean classes start up again or simply that meetings and activities suspended during the summer holiday season resume.

It also signals the resumption of packing and carrying lunches for families all over the province, a task that can easily become boring for both the maker and the taker.

It helps to plan ahead when it comes to packing lunches for the week. Leftovers such as a chicken leg from a dinner become the basis for a brown bag meal a day or two later.

Wash and refrigerate fresh vegetables on the weekend. Then they'll be ready to pop into lunches or for snacks on busy weekdays. Carrots, celery, pepper sticks, radishes, lettuce, cucumber, beans, broccoli and cauliflower are all great for this. A simple dip can be made with a plain yogurt base or a salad dressing.

Fresh fruit abounds at this time of year, so save the easy-to-store apples and bananas for later in the year. Offer fresh apricots and peaches, plums and late cherries in lunches while fresh, local fruit is still available.

If sandwiches with bread become boring, try serving pita breads stuffed with cheese, cold meats and vegetables; or tortillas spread with peanut butter or cream cheese and rolled up around lettuce, cucumbers and pepper slices.

Even whole wheat crackers with cheese cubes on the side can make a fun and different lunch for a change.

Some lunchers will have access to a microwave oven, where leftovers make a welcome reappearance. Casseroles, meat with gravy or a sauce, or spaghetti are all good candidates for re-heating deliciously.

Remember that even cookies may not withstand the rigours of junior's walk, skip, run or wrestle to school, so keep that in mind as you prepare for another season of brown-bagging it.

Late summer is also the time when the garden's bounty is overflowing, whether it's zucchini, tomatoes, peppers, apricots, apples, peaches, garlic or herbs.

Some keep and others don't. Some can be dried, canned, frozen or pickled to preserve their flavours for the winter ahead when fresh has a completely different meaning.

Lainie's Spicy Salsa

This is the best salsa I've ever tasted. It's medium-spicy, so if you like it hotter, add more jalapenos or hotter habaneros to yours. Little jars of it make fabulous gifts. Use as a dip for corn or tortilla chips, a filling for Spanish omelettes or in nachos (see recipe for Microwaved Natchos.) Use meaty plum-type tomatoes like Roma.

10 lb. (4.5 kg) plum-type tomatoes
7 large cloves garlic
1/4 c. (60 ml) fresh parsley
2 tbsp. (30 ml) fresh basil
1 tbsp. (15 ml) fresh oregano
3 large onions
1 red pepper
1 green pepper
3-6 jalapeno peppers
6 oz. (156 ml) tomato paste
1/3 c. (75 ml) brown sugar
1/2 c. (125 ml) vinegar
1 tbsp. (15 ml) salt
2 tsp. (10 ml) black pepper
1 tsp. (5 ml) cumin
1 tsp. (5 ml) chili powder
 a bit of cilantro

- Skin tomatoes. (Pour boiling water over them and the skins can be easily slipped off. Don't try and do them all at once.)
- Mince garlic and fresh herbs, chop tomatoes, onions and peppers. A food processor can be used. Add remaining ingredients and put it all in a large pot on medium heat. Cook down for three to four hours.
- Pack into pint jars and process in a boiling water bath for 20 minutes.
- Makes 10 pints.

See photograph on page **94**

TOP:
Smashed Meatballs in Pitas

WITH
Tzatziki: Green Yogurt Dip

Recipes on pages **89 & 88**

BOTTOM:
Winnie's Apricot Scones

Recipe on page **90**

TOP:
Lainie's Spicy Salsa
Recipe on page **92**

BOTTOM:
Chocolate Zucchini Loaf
Recipe on page **98**

TOP:
**Zucchini &
Tomato
Medley**

Recipe on
page **99**

BOTTON:
**Mom's
Apple
Coffee
Cake**

Recipe on
page **100**

TOP:
Pretty Pink Pears
Recipe on page **102**

BOTTOM:
Grape & Grain Muffins
Recipe on page **104**

Microwaved Nachos

This is a quick and easy recipe using the salsa you canned in the summer. It's a bit messy to eat, but a very tasty snack.

24 tortilla chips
1 c. (250 ml) salsa
1 c. (250 ml) cheddar
1/4 c. (60 ml) green peppers
1/4 c. (60 ml) green onions

- Arrange tortilla chips on a paper towel-lined plate, until it's completely covered. Dab salsa over all the chips, then sprinkle grated cheddar cheese all over the salsa. Garnish with minced green peppers and onions.
- Microwave on high for one to two minutes or until cheese is completely melted.
- Set in the middle of the table, and invite everyone to dive in.

Horiatiki/Greek Salad

Summer is the only time of year to make this, when the tomatoes, peppers, cukes and herbs are fresh from the garden. It's an explosion of wonderful, sunny flavours.

1/2 English cucumber
2 large tomatoes
1 sweet onion
2 green peppers
1/2 lb. (225 g) Greek feta cheese
1 tbsp. (15 ml) oregano
garnish with black Kalamata olives

DRESSING:
1/4 c. (60 ml) olive oil
2 tbsp. (30 ml) fresh lemon juice
1/2 tsp. (2 ml) cracked black pepper
sprinkle of sea salt

- Cut all vegetables into 1/2-inch cubes, and crumble, grate or cube feta over the top. Garnish with chopped fresh oregano or basil, or half that amount of dried herbs.
- Whisk together all the dressing ingredients, and pour over the salad, tossing gently to coat the fresh vegetables. You may not need all the dressing, but it will keep until you're ready for another one.
- Let the salad marinate for an hour or two before serving.
- Serves 4-6.

WINE FOR MICROWAVED NACHOS:
This really needs one of the many crisp lagers from our great microbreweries.

WINE FOR HORIATIKI/GREEK SALAD:
Greek cuisine always brings Retsina to mind – that famous dry resin-flavoured white that is so well adapted to Greek food. The closest we come to that in British Columbia is Silver Sage's Grand Sage, a dry Gewürztraminer infused with sage.

Zucchini Pancakes

These can be served for breakfast, with cheese, bacon or sausages, or as a vegetable dish with dinner. It's a great way to use the zucchini that got away under those big leaves and grew to two feet in length. Just discard the seedy centre if they're tough and grate the skin and flesh.

2 c. (500 ml) grated zucchini
1 small onion
1/2 c. (125 ml) whole wheat flour
1 tsp. (5 ml) baking powder
1 tsp. (5 ml) fresh tarragon
1/2 tsp. (2 ml) salt
1/2 tsp. (2 ml) pepper
1 egg

- Coarsely grate zucchini and chop onion finely.
- Whisk dry ingredients together and sprinkle over the vegetables.
- Mix thoroughly.
- Beat egg and add it to the mixture, blending well.
- Drop by spoonful onto greased frypan on medium-high heat, turning when they're browned.

Liz's Chocolate Zucchini Loaf

This delectable loaf makes an annual appearance at our house and everyone who's ever tried it has raved about it. This recipe makes two loaves so I always freeze one for when company drops in for coffee.

I have substituted chocolate chips for the walnuts, to good effect.

3/4 c. (175 ml) butter
1 1/2 c. (375 ml) sugar
3 eggs
2 1/2 c. (625 ml) flour
1/2 c. (125 ml) cocoa
1 tsp. (5 ml) salt
2 1/2 tsp. (12 ml) baking powder
1 1/2 tsp. (7 ml) baking soda
2 c. (500 ml) grated zucchini
1/2 c. (125 ml) milk
2 tsp. (10 ml) vanilla
1 c. (250 ml) chopped walnuts

- Pre-heat oven to 350 degrees F.
- Cream butter, sugar and eggs.
- Whisk dry ingredients together until they're well-mixed, then stir in the grated zucchini.
- Fold the zucchini mixture into the creamed ingredients.
- Add milk, vanilla and walnuts and mix well, then split the batter between two greased loaf pans.
- Sprinkle with chocolate chips or a few more chopped nuts and bake for one hour.

See photograph on page **94**

WINE FOR ZUCCHINI PANCAKES:
I would chill a full-flavoured white like Thornhaven's Sauvignon Blanc/ Chardonnay or Hester Creek's Sémillon/ Chardonnay.

Zucchini & Tomato Medley

This is a great way to serve, or pre-serve the over-abundance of tomatoes and zucchini at this time of year. Without the peppers, this freezes well for later in winter when the snow is flying over the tomato patch.

WINE FOR ZUCCHINI & TOMATO MEDLEY: *Either a fruity white, like Stag's Hollow's Tragically Vidal or Arrowleaf's Snow Tropics Vidal; or a rosé like Therapy's Pink Freud, or a lighter red like Red Rooster Pinot Noir.*

1 onion
1-2 cloves garlic
1 tbsp. (15 ml) olive oil
4 tomatoes
3 c. (750 ml) zucchini
1 c. (250 ml) peppers
2 tbsp. (30 ml) parsley
2 tsp. (10 ml) basil
1/2 tsp. (2 ml) thyme
1/2 tsp. (2 ml) pepper
1/4 tsp. (1 ml) salt

- Chop onion and mince garlic.
- Heat olive oil on medium in a wok or large frypan and saute onion and until soft. Add garlic for the last minute or two.
- Meanwhile, chop tomatoes and zucchini into one or two-inch chunks. (I add yellow scallop squash too if I have any.)
- Seed and chop colourful sweet peppers if you wish to add them.
- Mince fresh herbs.
- Add tomatoes to onion mixture, stirring and cooking until some of the liquid has evaporated, adding salt and pepper and minced herbs.
- Add remaining vegetables and combine well, then turn heat down to low, cover and simmer gently for an hour.
- This may be transferred to a casserole dish and baked in a 350 F oven for an hour instead.
- Serve when the vegetables are tender, sprinkled with fresh herbs.
- Omit peppers and freeze for a taste of summer in the coming winter months.
- Serves 4.

See photograph on page **95**

Sharon's Green Beans with Chillies

This recipe from a dear friend is a different and delightful way to spice up green beans when you're beginning to get tired of the fresh ones from the garden. Combined with fresh sweet peppers, this is an attractive and colourful dish to perk up jaded appetites.

1 garlic clove
1 small onion
drizzle of oil
1/2 lb. (227 g) green beans
1/2 red pepper
1/2 yellow pepper
2 tbsp. (30 ml) soy sauce
2 tbsp. (30 ml) sugar
1/4 tsp. (2 ml) chilli flakes

- Saute finely-chopped onion in a wok or frypan in a drizzle of oil until beginning to soften. Add garlic.
- String fresh green beans. Add them whole to the onion mixture and continue to stir. Slice peppers into strips and mix in with the beans.
- Combine soy, sugar and chilli flakes and add. Stir it all together and cook until beans are crisp-tender.
- Serves 4.

Mom's Apple Coffee Cake

Decadently delicious, but not too rich, this is excellent served for a coffee or tea party, a bridal shower or even for brunch.

1 large apple
3/4 c. (175 ml) brown sugar
1 egg
1/4 c. (60 ml) soft butter
1/2 c. (125 ml) skim milk
1 1/2 c. (375 ml) whole wheat flour
2 tsp. (10 ml) baking powder
1/2 tsp. (2 ml) salt

TOPPING:
1/2 c. (125 ml) brown sugar
2 tbsp. (30 ml) flour
2 tbsp. (30 ml) butter
2 tsp. (10 ml) cinnamon
1/2 c. (125 ml) chopped nuts

- Pre-heat oven to 375F.
- Grease and flour a nine-inch square pan.
- Peel and core one large or two small apples, then slice. Set aside.
- Thoroughly mix brown sugar, egg and butter.
- Stir in milk.
- Whisk together the whole wheat flour, baking powder and salt, then stir into wet ingredients.
- Spread in pan, then push the chunks of sliced apple into the batter, close together.
- Thoroughly combine topping ingredients, adding chopped nuts if you wish. Sprinkle the topping over it all as evenly as possible.
- Bake for 25 to 35 minutes.
- May be served warm.

See photograph on page **95**

Pat's Apple Chunky

Sweet and crunchy, this is ever-so-easy to make and is a favourite recipe in our family. It's excellent for bag lunches because there's no icing on top to make a mess. It's sweet enough as it is.

2 c. (500 ml) flour
2 tsp. (10 ml) baking powder
1 tsp. (5 ml) cinnamon
1/4 tsp. (1 ml) salt
1/2 c. (125 ml) butter
1 1/2 c. (375 ml) sugar
2 eggs
1 tsp. (5 ml) vanilla
1 c. (250 ml) apples
1 c. (250 ml) walnuts

- Pre-heat oven to 350F.
- Combine dry ingredients in a medium-sized bowl.
- In a large bowl, melt butter and stir in sugar, then cool.
- Beat in eggs and vanilla.
- Add all dry ingredients, then peeled, cored, chopped apples and chopped nuts, if desired.
- Stir well and press into a large baking pan (about 9x13 inches).
- Bake for 40-45 minutes.
- Cut into squares and serve.

WINE FOR APPLE SLAPS:
These desserts would pair nicely with Charmela, a Chardonnay/Apple dessert wine made by Mistaken Identity Vineyards.

Apple Slaps

These are crispy little rings with hearts of soft, sweet apple; delicious with a slice of bacon for breakfast or with grilled or roasted pork for supper. This recipe, although I've adapted it, came in a little book with my new Findlay Oval wood cook stove a few decades ago.

1/3 c. (75 ml) whole wheat flour
1/4 c. (60 ml) white flour
1 tsp. (5 ml) baking soda
1/2 tsp. (2 ml) cinnamon
1/2 tsp. (2 ml) salt
3-4 apples
1 egg
1/2 c. (125 ml) milk
1 tbsp. (15 ml) oil

- Mix flours, soda, cinnamon and salt.
- Core apples, and peel if you wish, then cut each one into about four or five rings.
- Beat egg and stir into flour mixture with milk and oil until dry ingredients are just moistened.
- Heat frypan over medium-high heat and add a dab of butter before dipping each ring in the batter and frying until brown. Turn over and brown the other side before serving.
- Repeat, adding butter to the pan as needed, browning all the apple rings, and using all the batter.
- Serves 3-4.

Pretty Pink Pears

These do look really pretty but best of all, they taste pretty yummy too. I leave the cores and the stem in for stability. Choose pears that aren't too ripe.

6 pears
1 knob of ginger
2 c. (500 m) red wine
1/2 c. (125 ml) honey
1 tbsp. (15 ml) lemon juice
1 cinnamon stick
1 chunk of orange peel
1 black peppercorn
1 clove
1 star anise

whipped cream
1 oz. (30 ml) brandy

- Slice a thin bit off the bottom of each pear so they sit up straight.
- Peel them. Scrape the peel off the ginger with a teaspoon and slice the ginger into strips.
- Combine a good red wine, like a shiraz, with all the other ingredients except the pears in a pot large enough to hold all the whole pears comfortably.
- Bring it to bubbling and add the pears, gently turning once to coat with the poaching liquid. Turn the heat down to a low simmer, cover and let simmer for a half hour or so, turning them over carefully part of the way through.
- Turn the heat off and let them cool in the poaching liquid.
- Remove the pears and store them in the fridge, then bring the poaching liquid back to simmering, reducing it to a thick glaze.
- To serve, mound whipped cream, sweetened with a little brandy, in a shallow bowl and nest each pear in it. Drizzle each fruit with the red wine glaze.
- Serves 6.

See photograph on page **96**

WINE FOR PRETTY PINK PEARS:
This deserves a good red Icewine, like the Jackson-Triggs Cabernet Franc Icewine or Mt. Boucherie's Pinot Noir Icewine or Willow Hill's Merlot Icewine.

Pear & Ginger Chutney

This makes a delicious condiment to serve with curries, roasted meats, or as part of your ploughman's lunch, with a slab of fresh bread and a hearty cheddar.

4 c. (1 l) pears
1 small onion
1/4 c. (60 ml) preserved ginger
1 c. (250 ml) raisins
1/2 c. (125 ml) vinegar
1/4 c. (60 ml) lemon juice
2 tsp. (10 ml) salt
1 tsp. (5 ml) allspice
1/2 tsp. (2 ml) cinnamon
1/2 tsp. (2 ml) cloves
1/2 tsp. (2 ml) ground ginger
3/4 c. (175 ml) dark brown sugar
1 57-g box Certo powdered pectin
4 1/2 c. (1.125 ml) sugar

- Prepare the pears by peeling and coring about three pounds. Cut them up into small pieces. You should have four cups of fruit. Chop onion. Drain and sliver pieces of ginger.
- Dump it all into a very large pot and add the remaining ingredients except sugar and pectin.
- Stir well over high heat until the mixture comes to a hard boil.
- Stir in sugars and pectin, and bring back to a full rolling boil, stirring constantly at that hard boil for five minutes.
- Remove from heat and skim off any foam with a metal spoon.
- Stir for 10 minutes to cool slightly and to prevent floating fruit in the finished chutney.
- Ladle quickly into sterilized jars and cover with a layer of hot paraffin wax about an eighth inch thick.

Grape and Grain Muffins

These are reminiscent of the warm johnnycake my Mom made occasionally for dessert served with melted honey drizzled over it. Don't tell anyone, but these might be good for you too. The Okanagan Valley's virtually-seedless Coronation grapes are fabulous in baked goods.

1 c. (250 ml) cornmeal
3/4 c. (175 ml) whole wheat flour
1/3 c. (75 ml) rolled oats
1/4 c. (60 ml) oat bran
1 1/2 tsp. (8 ml) baking soda
1 c. (250 ml) buttermilk
1 tbsp. (15 ml) honey
1 egg
1/4 c. (60 ml) oil
1 c. (250 ml) Coronation grapes

- Pre-heat oven to 400 F.
- Combine dry ingredients and mix well. You may substitute a further quarter cup of flour for the oat bran if you wish.
- Whip wet ingredients together and add to the dry ones, stirring together quickly until everything is well-combined.
- Fold in grapes and spoon into greased muffin cups.
- Bake for 15 to 20 minutes, watching for browning.
- This makes 12 small but crunchy, hearty muffins with bursts of sweetness from the grapes.

See photograph on page 96

Mom's Dill Pickles

Everyone always raves over Mom's dills, so I thought I should share her recipe.

3 lb. (1.5 kg) small cucumbers
fresh dillweed
cloves of garlic
cherry leaves
1 qt. (1 l) cider vinegar
3 c. (750 ml) water
1 c. (250 ml) coarse salt

- Wash pickling cucumbers and prick each one all around with a fork.
- Sterilize jars and sealing lids. Pack jars, adding a clump of dill, a clove of garlic and a cherry leaf to each.
- Bring vinegar, water and salt to a boil and fill each jar with the hot liquid.
- Seal, and let stand for at least six weeks.
- Makes about five or six pint jars.

Grape & Wine Jelly with Jalapenos

My friend Winnie and I made this grape jelly with some mystery grapes the bear left one year to ripen on my one vine, and we thought jalapeno peppers would give it a tasty kick. So we added minced hot peppers as well as a little wine. We like wine.

Turns out it's great dabbed on cream cheese on a cracker or with grilled meats, or on toast.

6 c. (1.5 l) grape juice
1/2 c. (125 ml) pinot grigio wine
4 1/2 c. (1.25 l) sugar
1 49-g box Certo light pectin crystals
3 jalapenos, minced

- Stem and thoroughly crush five to six pounds of white grapes. Put in a large pot.
- Add two cups water and bring to a boil; simmer, covered, 10 minutes and extract juice using a jelly bag and letting it drip through overnight.
- In another large pot, stir together over high heat, the juice, a quarter cup of the measured sugar and the Certo light pectin crystals.
- Bring to a boil, then add the rest of the sugar. Return to a hard boil for one minute.
- Remove from heat. Stir in minced seeded jalapenos and skim the liquid for five minutes to remove foam. If you're not keen on the colour, add a few drops of green or yellow food colouring.
- Pour into warm sterilized jars to within a quarter-inch of the rim.
- Wipe rim, cover with lids and screw rings on tightly.
- Process for five minutes in a boiling water bath or top with paraffin.

See photograph on page **129**

Autumn

9. Slow Cooking/Fast Food

PLANNED-OVERS

September spells the end of vacations and summer fun. Life speeds up for most families, with a return to classes, evening meetings, courses, sports and other activities, so healthy meals that can be prepared quickly are like solid gold.

If you can organize your mornings to include a few minutes of preparation, the slow cooker is a gem in the kitchen, allowing everyone to arrive home to the delicious smells of a home-cooked meal at the end of the day.

Doing a bit of extra preparation on days off is another way to save time between school or work and a busy evening.

A third option, without resorting to the drive-thru or frozen dinners, is to double the recipe on a night when there's a little more time, and serve it a second time a couple of days later – but with a fresh face.

For instance, a steak dinner can become a steak salad later in the week. Just add thinly sliced mushrooms, cucumber and tomatoes to a pile of fresh greens such as baby spinach or other salad leaves.

Thinly slice the leftover steak over it and add a scattering of sunflower seeds. That piece of meat, which can be a lower-priced blade or round steak which has been marinated before grilling, serves double duty and provides you with two quick meals.

Similarly, baked or grilled chicken makes a nice meal for the family on the night when you have an hour for it to spend in the oven, then it can be trotted out again, slivered cold, for a quick meal later in the week – on top of a pile of healthy greens.

Then there are the dishes which naturally make leftovers without any changes. Casseroles, spaghetti and meatballs, stews and roasts are tasty the first time and they reheat as an encore meal without losing their flavour and texture.

Make extra, so you've got that second meal in the bag. Think ahead to the sort of weekend meals you can make that will also provide you with a satisfying repeat performance, later in the week, when life's a little more hectic.

For the slow cooker, look for less expensive cuts of beef that require long, gentle cooking to tenderize them: cross rib or chuck blade roasts, round steaks or sirloin tip. They are fairly lean and can be easily cut up for stewing – or buy stew meat, already cubed.

It's not easy to come up with delicious, nutritious, quick meals every day for a family, but a little advance planning and preparation can be rewarding down the line.

Sunday Pot Roast Plus

This makes a flavourful dinner the first day, and it's just like a new dinner the second. You may substitute water for the wine, or half apple juice and half water.

WINE FOR SUNDAY POT ROAST PLUS: *This calls for a big red blend with character, like Misconduct's The Big Take or Therapy's Freud's Ego*

3 lb. (1.5 kg) beef pot roast
salt, pepper and flour
2 onions
2 garlic cloves
4 large carrots
2 celery stalks
drizzle of oil
1 c. (250 ml) beef stock
1 c. (250 ml) red wine
1 tbsp. (15 ml) Worcestershire
3 cloves
1 inch cinnamon stick
12 peppercorns
2 tbsp.(30 ml) cornstarch
3 tbsp. (45 ml) cold water

- Dredge a beef roast such as cross rib, blade, shoulder or brisket in salt, pepper and flour.
- Cut onions into about eight wedges each; smash garlic cloves and chop coarsely. Cut carrots and celery into chunks.
- Brown floured meat quickly over medium-high heat in a Dutch oven in a drizzle of oil. Remove it and soften the onions in the same pot.
- Add minced garlic,stock, wine, Worcestershire sauce, cloves, cinnamon stick, peppercorns and vegetables.
- Bring to bubbling and return the roast, turning it over in the liquid to coat.
- Turn to lowest possible stove temperature or pop it into the oven at about 325 F for a couple of hours, covered.
- After two or three hours, remove the roast and let it rest, covered in foil, for a few minutes while you fish out the vegetables and put them into a serving dish. Keep them warm while you thicken the juices. Stir the cornstarch into the cold water. When the juices are bubbling on the stove, add the cornstarch mix and whisk it in until it thickens and turns translucent.
- Remove from heat and serve the sliced roast and drained vegetables, with the gravy on the side.
- Substitute or add such vegetables as mushrooms, parsnips, turnips or potatoes to this, along with the carrots and celery, or serve broccoli or other vegetables on the side.
- It's good with boiled potatoes.
- Serves 8 or so or 4 with leftovers.

Second Day Pot Roast

They'll never know this is the same meat you cooked a couple of days previous.

leftover pot roast, as above
leftover sauce, as above
2 c. (500 ml) frozen peas
4 green onions
6 mushrooms
2 c. (500 ml) pasta

■ Dice pot roast. Reheat the diced meat in the sauce in the microwave. Add water if needed to achieve the right consistency.
■ Thinly slice mushrooms and add with peas and green onions and heat it all through.
■ Cook pasta. Use fusilli or corkscrew pasta, or shells. Whole wheat varieties are healthy choices.
■ Pour meat, veggies and sauce over pasta and serve.

Beef in Beer

This is one of our favourites recipes, and I've heard the same comment from many others. This appeared in one of my first food columns. It's great done either on the stove top or in the slow cooker.

2 lb. (1 kg) beef strips or cubes
flour, salt and pepper
skim of oil
1-2 large onion(s), sliced
1-4 cloves of garlic, crushed
4-6 carrots
2 ribs celery
12 mushrooms, whole
1 1/2 c. (355 ml) beer
1 tsp. (5 ml) brown sugar

■ Dredge beef chuck, round or other stewing meat in flour seasoned with salt and pepper to taste.
■ Slice onions, crush garlic, chop up carrots, celery and mushrooms, if large.
■ Heat enough oil over medium heat, to coat the bottom of a dutch oven or heavy pot, and saute onions until limp, but not brown.
■ Remove onions and add enough oil to thinly cover the bottom of the pot, and brown the beef.
■ Return onions to the pot, along with minced or crushed garlic and vegetables.
■ Stir in beer and sugar.
■ Bring it back to bubbling, then lower heat, cover and simmer for two hours or so, or put it into a 325 F oven for the same time. Or, you can cook it in the slow cooker for about eight hours.
■ Serves 6.

WINE FOR SECOND DAY POT ROAST: *The pasta puts me in the mood for something Italian, like Sandhill's Barbera, or something Austrian like Mt. Boucherie's Zweigelt.*

WINE FOR BEEF IN BEER: *Have a big Syrah, like Nichol or Marichel, although I might also take my cue from the recipe and pour a bitter ale.*

Denny's Hunter's Stew

The smells make your mouth water as this is cooking. It's a wonderful greeting for visitors or family who've been active outside in cooler weather. Serve with boiled potatoes, pasta or fresh bread or rolls.

This heats up really well for a quick second meal a couple of days later. This could be a stew, a roast or a steak dinner.

3 lb. (1.4 kg) meat
seasoned flour mixture
skim of oil
2 cloves garlic
28 oz. (796 ml) tomatoes
6 peppercorns
1 tbsp. (15 ml) fresh oregano
1 tsp. (5 ml) fresh tarragon
1 tsp. (5 ml) fresh basil
6 small onions
2 ribs celery
12 carrots
8 mushrooms

WINE FOR DENNY'S HUNTER'S STEW: *This calls for a hearty red like a Syrah from Herder, Camelot Vineyard or Quinta Ferreira. wines.*

- Pre-heat oven to 325 F.
- Choose simmering cuts of roast or steak, or stew meat, either beef or a game such as venison or moose. In fact, you could cook a chicken and call it cacciatore...
- Dredge the meat in flour seasoned with salt and pepper, then brown in a large oven-safe pot or Dutch oven in a skim of oil, adding chopped garlic near the end.
- Add tin of tomatoes, chopped herbs and other seasonings. Stir and bring the mixture to a boil before covering and putting in the oven for three hours or so in total.
- For the last hour or two of cooking, add the small whole onions, or large, chopped ones; chopped celery, pieces of carrot and whole mushrooms.
- Vary the vegetables to your taste.
- If the meat is eaten and just tomatoes and vegetables are left use the sauce as a base for soup the next day, or for a pasta sauce.
- Serves 8-10.

Arla's Spicy Beef Stew

This is suitable for those who cannot eat wheat, because it's thickened with cornmeal instead of flour. It's excellent cooked in a slow cooker all day, then thickened at the end. It heats up deliciously for a second meal a couple of days later.

2 lb. (1 kg) lean beef
drizzle of oil
1 onion, sliced
2 cloves of garlic, minced
2 1/2 c. (625 ml) beef or chicken broth
2 tsp. (10 ml) dried oregano
1 tsp. (5 ml) cumin powder
1 tsp. (5 ml) salt
1 tbsp. (15 ml) minced jalapeno
     peppers
4 to 6 carrots, sliced
1 or 2 stalks of celery, sliced
2 tbsp. (30 ml) cornmeal

- Trim meat and cube it or cut it into thick strips.
- Heat oil in a Dutch oven and brown the meat and onion, adding the minced garlic, then the broth, herbs and spices, except the hot peppers. (You could leave them out if you'd prefer.)
- Add sliced carrots and celery.
- Bring to bubbling, then reduce the heat to low and simmer for a couple of hours, either on the stove or in a medium oven.
- When the meat is tender, stir in minced jalapeno peppers and cornmeal and bring back to bubbling, simmering for a half hour longer, until the sauce is nice and thick.
- This could also be cooked in a slow cooker all day on low, then the peppers and cornmeal added for the last half-hour of cooking.
- This is good served on squares of cornbread or on brown rice.
- Serves 6 to 8.

WINE FOR ARLA'S SPICY BEEF STEW: *This calls again for a hearty red blend, like Quinta Ferreira's Mistura Tinto or See Ya Later Ranch's Ping or Cerelia's Misceo.*

Chicken with Veggies & Basil

This can be thrown together when you're half-asleep in the morning before work, and it will welcome you home later in the day. Or, the meat and vegetables could be prepared the night before and it would then only take five minutes to assemble the meal in the slow cooker before leaving for work.

6 chicken pieces
3 carrots
2 celery stalks
2 garlic cloves
6 plum tomatoes
2 med. onions
1 tbsp. (15 ml) basil pesto
fresh-ground black pepper, to taste
salt, to taste
1/4 c. (60 ml) dry white wine

WINE FOR CHICKEN WITH VEGGIES & BASIL: *This calls for a white with the flavours and the mineral backbone to stand up to this hearty dish, such as the Roussanne-Marsanne blends from Moon Curser or Inniskillin Okanagan.*

- Skin chicken pieces. Scrub and trim carrots and celery. Skin and chop tomatoes. (I used frozen ones from last summer's garden, but you could substitute a tin of squashed or whole tomatoes.) Squash and coarsely chop garlic. Skin onions and chop into four to six wedges.
- Toss vegetables into slow cooker, lay chicken pieces on top, then sprinkle basil pesto, (substitute fresh basil or dried, if necessary. I use a frozen dab from last summer's garden.) Spread chopped tomatoes on top and sprinkle with freshly-ground black pepper and a sprinkle of salt.
- Drizzle a little wine over top.
- Cover and turn the slow cooker to low.
- Leave, covered, for eight to 10 hours.

Slow-cooked Polynesian Pork

This is an easy dinner with an exotic flavour that cooks while you're out playing or working. It will perfume the whole house. To complete the meal just steam a few vegetables such as turnips, parsnips, carrots or brussels sprouts. Serve over rice, pasta or boiled potatoes.

1 lb. (454 g) pork
drizzle of oil
2 onions
1 garlic clove
1 tbsp. (15 ml) sesame seeds
2 tbsp. (30 ml) soy sauce
1 tbsp. (15 ml) molasses
1 tbsp. (15 ml) balsamic vinegar
2 tsp. (10 ml) minced fresh ginger
1/4 tsp. (1 ml) cayenne pepper
1/2 c. (125 ml) water

1 tbsp. (15 ml) cornstarch
1 tbsp. (15 ml) cold water

- Trim fat from pork and cut into one-inch cubes. Brown lightly in a frypan drizzled with a little oil, then dump into the bottom of the slow cooker.
- Slice onions, mince garlic and add onion to frypan from which you removed the pork. Soften, stirring often, then toss in the remaining ingredients.
- Pour over the top of the meat in the slow cooker.
- Cover and turn to low, leaving the lid on, for six to eight hours.
- Turn up to high, combine cornstarch and cold water in a small bowl, then stir in to liquid in slow cooker. Cover and leave for 15 minutes or so, to thicken the sauce.
- Serves 4.

WINE FOR SLOW-COOKED POLYNESIAN:
I would pour myself a glass of Pinot Noir; say from Mt. Boucherie, Arrowleaf, Quails' Gate, CedarCreek, Nk'Mip or Seven Stones.

Bill's Texas Barbecue Pot Roast

This slow-cooked dinner is rich in flavour, but lean on the pocketbook. It's easy to prepare in less than a half hour before and after work. Try this with Slow-Cooker Dumplings, page 116.

WINE FOR BILL'S TEXAS BARBECUE POT ROAST: *I'd like a bold and juicy red, like See Ya Later Ranch Rover or Herder Merlot or Tinhorn Creek's 2Bench Red.*

3 lb. (1.5 kg) cross rib roast
drizzle of oil
1 lg. onion
1 clove garlic
4 carrots
6 mushrooms
8 oz. (125 ml) tomato sauce
2 tbsp. (30 ml) brown sugar
3 tbsp. (45 ml) cider vinegar
1 tbsp. (15 ml) Worcestershire
1 tbsp. (15 ml) dried oregano
1 tsp. (5 ml) dried basil
1 tsp. (5 ml) salt
1/2 tsp. (2 ml) pepper
pinch of cayenne pepper

- Trim fat and brown the beef in a Dutch oven or a deep frypan in a drizzle of oil. Any pot roast could be substituted for the cross rib.
- You could also eliminate the browning step and put all the ingredients directly into the pot, but the flavour's much better when the meat is browned first.
- Remove to slow cooker and soften chopped onion and minced garlic in the first pot, in another drizzle of oil over medium heat.
- Put into slow cooker, along with chopped carrots and mushrooms (leave them whole if not too large).
- Combine remaining ingredients in a bowl or measuring cup and pour over meat and vegetables in slow cooker.
- Cook on low for 8-10 hours without lifting the lid.
- Serves 4 to 6.

Beef Stew with Wine

This makes a quick and easy meal for when you'll be out all day, but want to come home to a meal that makes the whole house smell yummy. Double the recipe to make enough for a second meal.

1 lb. (454 g) stew beef
2 tbsp. (30 ml) flour
salt and pepper, to taste
drizzle of oil
1 c. (250 ml) beef broth
4 carrots
2 celery stalks
1 onion
1 garlic clove
1/4 c. (60 ml) red wine
2 tsp. (10 ml) fresh thyme
1 tsp. (5 ml) fresh tarragon
1 tbsp. (15 ml) fresh parsley

- Dredge cubes of beef in a mixture of flour, salt and pepper and brown quickly in a little hot oil, then put into crockpot or slow cooker. Pour beef broth into the pan and scrape in any browned bits.
- Chop vegetables into chunks and mince garlic. Add to beef.
- Add beef broth, wine and herbs.
- Cover and simmer on low for 8 hours or so.
- Garnish with fresh chopped parsley. Serves 4.

Slow-cooker Dumplings

These are light and delicious, cooked in the juices which accumulate from the meat and vegetables that cooked all day in the slow cooker.

3/4 c. (175 ml) flour
1/2 c. (125 ml) cornmeal
2 tsp. (10 ml) baking powder
1 tsp. (5 ml) salt
2/3 c. (150 ml) milk
2 tbsp. (30 ml) oil

- Turn slow cooker up to high and remove roast to a board or platter, covering with foil to keep it warm.
- Mix dry ingredients together well, and beat milk with oil in a separate bowl or measuring cup.
- Stir dry and moist ingredients together, then arrange in six spoon-fuls, over top of vegetables and liquid remaining in slow cooker, close the lid and cook for 30 minutes longer, without peeking.
- Serve dumplings, vegetables and gravy over slices of roast beef.
- Serves 4 to 6.

WINE FOR BEEF STEW WITH WINE: *The aptly named Big Bang from Blasted Church is the red for this dish, although most blended reds will give you a lot of satisfaction.*

Parsley & Thyme Biscuit Topping

This savoury biscuit crust turns leftover beef stew into a pot pie.

3/4 c. (175 ml) flour
1/4 c. (60 ml) whole wheat flour
2 tsp. (10 ml) baking powder
1 tbsp. (15 ml) brown sugar
1/2 tsp. (2 ml) salt
1/4 tsp. (1 ml) black pepper
2 tbsp. (30 ml) fresh parsley
1 tsp. (5 ml) fresh thyme
2 tbsp. (30 ml) olive oil
1/3 c. (75 ml) milk

- Mix dry ingredients with a whisk and add minced fresh parsley and thyme.
- Combine olive oil and milk with the dry ingredients in a few quick strokes.
- Squeeze dough or knead it a dozen times, then pat out to a half-inch thickness and cut into rounds, or just dab onto top of hot stew.
- Bake, uncovered, at 425 F for about 15 minutes, or until the topping is nicely browned.
- Serves 2-4.

WINE FOR GROUSE WITH GRAPES: Viognier is a white wine with a little tannin which is why it would be such a good pairing here. Look for examples from Silkscarf, Quinta Ferreira and La Frenz.

Grouse with Grapes

The grapes and wine keep the delicate breast meat moist and flavourful.

If you don't have a grouse breast, use whatever other poultry is available. One large half chicken breast is about the equivalent of a whole grouse breast. This is delicious over a brown and wild rice pilaf. The Okanagan's home-bred Coronation grapes are delectable in this.

1 onion
drizzle of oil
2 grouse breasts
1/2 c. (125 ml) white wine
1 c. grapes (250 ml)
2 tsp. (10 ml) fresh tarragon
2 tsp. (10 ml) fresh parsley
1/2 tsp. (2 ml) salt
1/4 tsp. (1 ml) pepper

- Soften a chopped onion in a drizzle of oil in a non-stick pan over medium-high heat.
- Push them to the side and brown the breasts on both sides.
- Add dry white wine, grapes, fresh herbs and salt and pepper.
- Cover and simmer on low heat for 10-15 minutes until the breast is just cooked through but some liquid remains in the pan.
- Serves 2.

Moussaka with Merlot

My friend Sharon used to figure it was called Moose-aka because we always made it with ground moose meat, but it's not bad with lean ground beef either. Traditionally, ground lamb would be used in Greece, where this originated.

Historically, this would be made using eggplant, but you can substitute zucchini or potato for some or all of it, as I always do.

1 medium zucchini
1 medium eggplant
2 medium potatoes
sprinkle of salt
1 large onion
2 garlic cloves
skim of olive oil
1 lb. (454 g) ground meat
5.5 oz. (156 ml) tomato paste
1/2 c. (125 ml) red wine
2 tbsp. (30 ml) fresh parsley
1 tbsp. (15 ml) fresh oregano
1/2 tsp. (2 ml) cinnamon
salt and pepper to taste
1/2 c. (125 ml) parmesan
1/2 c. (125 ml) mozzarella
2 c. (500 ml) medium white sauce
1/2 tsp. (2 ml) nutmeg
white pepper and salt, to taste

- Peel and slice zucchini and eggplant in half-inch thick slices and slice two medium potatoes into quarter-inch thick slices.
- Sprinkle salt over eggplant slices and surround with paper towels to absorb the moisture.
- Meanwhile, chop onion and mince garlic and saute in a skim of olive oil in a large non-stick pan until limp.
- Add ground moose or lean ground beef (lamb is often used traditionally in Greece), breaking it up and stirring until browned.
- Add the tin of tomato paste, a robust red wine such as merlot, fresh, chopped herbs and spices, and let simmer, uncovered, for 15 minutes or so, stirring occasionally until it has absorbed all the liquid. Remove from heat.
- Lightly oil a large non-stick pan and quickly fry all the vegetable slices until they're just browned. (This may also be done under the broiler).
- Lay the eggplant slices on the bottom of a 9x12-inch casserole dish; cover with half the meat mixture and grated parmesan cheese.
- Lay zucchini on top, then remaining meat mixture and grated mozzarella cheese.
- Place potatoes or remaining eggplant on top, then spread a medium thick white sauce, seasoned with nutmeg, white pepper and salt, all over the top.
- Traditionally, for extra richness, two or three egg yolks would be beaten into the sauce at the end, but I don't add that.
- Bake at 350 F for 45 minutes to one hour. Let it rest for 10 minutes before cutting into squares and serving.
- Serves 8 or so.

WINE FOR MOUSSAKA WITH MERLOT:
If there is Merlot in the recipe, have a bottle on the table. B.C. makes terrific Merlot. Try Burrowing Owl, Jackson-Triggs, Church & State, LaStella, Herder, Orofino ... well, the list really goes on and most taste great.

10. Giving Thanks

THE BIG BIRD

Everyone can find some reason to be thankful at Thanksgiving, whether for a bountiful harvest, or for other blessings.

It's a time to mark the conclusion of the growing season and harvest a variety of summer's produce here in B.C., but it's also a time to reflect on the importance of family.

Although babies spit up, they also giggle with infectious glee; little kids break things, but they're also pretty good at heart-warmingly impulsive hugs; teens can be prickly, but there are also those exciting glimpses of innocence, combined with a new maturity.

Beyond that, family members are those you can share experiences, memories, feelings and opinions with. No one knows you like your family does, so there's no pretence allowed. No one forgives like family, because it's blood that binds, not just the occasional meeting for social reasons.

And, with children and grandchildren, nieces and nephews, we have these hopes and ambitions for them, along with a desire to be 'there' for them.

Large families can be a bit cumbersome, and it's a little frantic to get everyone together – but what a joy, too.

So, gather whatever family means to you, over a delicious meal. Get caught up on their news, and say thanks.

Share the bounty of local gardens and create more of those important memories that keep us going from one gathering to the next.

Give thanks, not just for the bounty of food, but also the bounty of family and friends.

Consider what it would be like without one or the other, or both.

For those to whom preparing a large turkey would result in an endless supply of leftovers, choose a chicken, a game hen or just part of the turkey.

Wherever you are, enjoy the company of family and friends and give thanks for that too.

Poultry Stuffing with Pork & Onion

The rule of thumb is to allow about half cup of dressing per pound of bird, so adjust these quantities to the size of bird you want to stuff.

This is quite a flavorful dressing, but you could leave out the sausage if you wanted it less rich. Whether or not you add some cashews, pine nuts or other nuts is up to you, but we like them.

2 links of pork sausage
2 c. (500 ml) onions
1 c. (250 ml) celery
1 apple
3-4 c. (750-900ml) dry bread
    crumbs
1/4 c. (60 ml) dry sherry
3 tbs. (45 ml) chopped fresh sage
1 tbsp. (15 ml) fresh parsley
1/2 tsp. (2 ml) rosemary
1/2 tsp. (2 ml) thyme
1/2 tsp. (2 ml) tarragon
1/4 c. (60 ml) cashews
fresh ground pepper and salt to taste

- Slice lean pork sausages up finely and fry up in a pan or wok, along with chopped-up onions and celery.
- Add a bit of oil if necesary to keep everything from sticking, and stir constantly until the meat is cooked and the vegetables are soft. Core an apple, chop it up and mix it in.
- Turn off the heat and add bread cubes, then drizzle sherry, apple juice or chicken broth over it all.
- Mince and add fresh sage, or half as much dried sage, other herbs (fresh if possible), and salt and pepper, to taste. Toss in some nuts and stir everything thoroughly.
- Lightly stuff cavity of bird just before you put it into the oven – not before.
- If you make the stuffing ahead of time, chill it immediately and keep it in the fridge until you're ready to put it into the bird.

WINE FOR POULTRY STUFFING WITH PORK & ONION: *A big turkey dinner involves so many guests and presents so many flavours that a choice of wines can be offered. I like a good dry Gewürztraminer or Viognier because I prefer the white meat. The dark meat and the dressing need a full-bodied Pinot Noir, like Kettle Valley, or a ripe Merlot, like Nk'Mip or Young & Wyse.*

Turkey Fried Rice

Some of us prefer leftover turkey to the first time it made its grand entrance.

2 carrots
1 onion
1 stalk celery
1 small zucchini
2 c. (500 ml) cooked turkey
2 tbsp. (30 ml) red pepper
2 tbsp. (30 ml) soy sauce
1/2 tsp. (2 ml) sugar
1/4 tsp. (1 ml) cayenne
1/4 c. (60 ml) water
4 c. cooked rice

- Sliver the vegetables and leftover turkey meat, arranging them on your cutting board.
- Heat a drizzle of cooking oil over medium-high heat in a large frypan or wok. Stir-fry onions and carrots, the vegetables which will take the longest time to cook first; then the celery and zucchini. Stir in the meat and red pepper last.
- Add the soy sauce, sugar and cayenne, along with enough water to steam it.
- Cover with a lid for just a minute or two.
- Then re-heat the rice by stir-frying it into the mixture, taste for seasoning and adjust as necessary.
- When the rice is completely heated through, spoon onto a serving platter.
- Serves 4.

WINE FOR TURKEY FRIED RICE: Leftovers suggest keeping the lid on the wine budget. Gray Monk's Latitude 50 wines – red, white and rosé – deliver good taste at affordable prices.

WINE FOR BROWN & WILD RICE PILAF: I would serve a Vancouver Island Pinot Gris – Averill Creek, Garry Oaks, Blue Grouse, for instance – or one of the white blends from Venturi-Schulze because the bright acidity and piquant flavours will go well with this dish.

Brown & Wild Rice Pilaf

This is a great combination of colourful vegetables and different kinds of rice. Use it as a filling side dish or a vegetarian meal in itself. Vary the vegetables according to what you have available fresh.

1 onion
1 stalk celery
1 large carrot
1 tbsp. (15 ml) butter
1 tsp. (5 ml) cumin
1/4 tsp. (2 ml) salt
1 c. (250 ml) brown rice
1/2 c. (125 ml) wild rice
2 c. (500 ml) fresh spinach
3 c. (750 ml) chicken stock
1/2 c. (125 ml) peas

- Chop onion, celery and carrot and soften in melted butter over medium heat, in a medium-sized pot. Add cumin and salt.
- Rinse rice and add to the vegetables, stirring well. Rinse and chop fresh spinach. Mix in well. (Substitute chopped chard if available and add a few mushrooms if you have some around).
- Add boiling chicken stock, stir, cover and lower the heat to simmer gently for 40 minutes, without peeking.
- Add frozen or fresh peas, cover and cook for a further five minutes or until rice is cooked to your taste.
- Serves 4.

Turkey in Curry Sauce

One good reason to roast a turkey is having it to serve a day or two later in a curry-flavoured sauce. Even the kids always enjoy this. It's not a hot curry, although you could adjust the spices to suit your taste. Serve it spooned over pasta, rice or toast.

1 large onion
oil
3 ribs celery
1 carrot
4 mushrooms
1 green pepper or peas
2 c. (500 ml) cooked turkey
2 tbsp. (30 ml) butter
2 tbsp. (30 ml) flour
1 c. (250 ml) milk
1 tsp. (5 ml) curry
salt and pepper to taste

- Chop onion, celery, carrot, mushrooms, pepper and turkey.
- Saute chopped onion in a large frypan in a little oil, adding mushrooms, celery and carrot coins and stirring over medium heat for several minutes until the onion is translucent.
- Add the peppers and turkey and stir gently until heated through.
- Remove the vegetables and meat to your serving dish, and melt the butter over medium heat. Add flour and stir well, cooking for about a minute, before slowly whisking in the milk. Continue to beat until it thickens and is smooth, tipping the pan if necessary to whisk out all the lumps.
- The white sauce could be made separately if you prefer. Season with salt, pepper and as much of a good curry powder as you like.
- Return the meat and vegetables to the sauce and reheat, stirring carefully but thoroughly.
Serves 4.

WINE FOR TURKEY IN CURRY SAUCE: *Contrary to conventional opinion, I never recommend Gewürztraminer with curry because the spice flavours compete. I prefer a crisp Pinot Blanc, like those from Hester Creek, Red Rooster and Dunham & Froese.*

Butter-browned Carrots & Parsnips

Everyone loves carrots, but if there was any question, this will cinch it. I never seem to make enough to satisfy the whole crew. Remember, though, if you increase the amount of vegetables, only increase the water a smidge because that dictates how long they will cook.

1 c. (250 ml) parsnips
1 c. (250 ml) carrots
2 tbsp. (30 ml) butter
1/2 tsp. (2 ml) fresh ginger
1 tbsp. (15 ml) brown sugar
1 tsp. (5 ml) lemon juice
1/2 c. (125 ml) boiling water

sprinkling of salt
garnish of green onions or herbs

- Peel and trim a couple of parsnips and three or four carrots, cut into sticks about 1/4-inch square and two to three inches long. At this point, they can be prepared ahead and bundled up in a plastic bag in the fridge until a half-hour or so before dinner.
- Melt butter in a frypan or Dutch oven with a tight lid, add the parsnips, carrots, minced ginger, brown sugar, lemon juice, boiling water and salt.
- Stir the vegetables about until they're well-mixed and the water has returned to a boil. Cover tightly, and reduce heat to medium.
- Cook until the water evaporates, then allow them to brown in the butter before serving. Keep an eye on them so they don't burn.
- Sprinkle with fresh chopped green onion tops or herbs such as chives or parsley.
- Serves 3-4.

Braided Bread with Cheese & Onion

This bread looks good and tastes even better. It's simpler to form than you would think. You just need to know how to braid.

1 1/2 c. (375 ml) warm water
1/2 c. (125 ml) warm milk
2 tbsp. (30 ml) dry yeast
2 tbsp. (30 ml) melted butter
1/4 c. (60 ml) honey
2 tbsps (30 ml) green onion
1 1/2 tsp. (8 ml) black pepper
1 tsp. (5 ml) salt
1 egg
3 c. (750 ml) whole wheat flour
3 c. (750 ml) white flour
1 1/2 c. (375 ml) sharp cheddar
sesame seeds, to garnish

- Heat water and milk to 100 C to 115 C in a large warmed bowl and sprinkle with two packages of regular yeast or two spoonfuls of bulk dry yeast. Stir in.
- Add melted butter or margarine to the liquid. Stir in honey until it has dissolved.
- Mince green onion and add along with salt and pepper. Beat an egg and stir in.
- Begin adding flour, one cup at a time, mixing each cup in before adding another.
- The mixture will be so stiff it's difficult to mix with a wooden spoon.

- Dig in with your hands when the dough is firm, and turn out onto a floured board.
- Begin kneading the dough, pulling the top part of the dough into the middle and leaning heavily into it, turning it a quarter turn and repeating the rhythmic turn, fold and knead. The dough will change under your hands. Have a little pile of extra flour beside your work area and sprinkle more on the work surface or your hands, if needed.
- One of the most fascinating parts of bread-making is watching the change that takes place in the dough as you knead. You can be very assertive, releasing all your aggressions in a beneficial way.
- It should take about 10 or even 12 minutes until the dough is smooth and satiny and no longer sticks to the board or your fingers.
- I use an oil spray to lightly coat the mixing bowl. Set the dough ball smooth-side down, then turn it over to grease it. Cover with a towel.
- Set aside in a warm place (85 F is ideal) to rise until it's doubled in size, about 45 minutes to an hour.
- In the meantime, grate the cheddar, ready to knead it in later.
- Turn the dough out onto a lightly floured board and punch it down hard, so it completely loses its puffiness.

CONTINUED ON PAGE 125

CONTINUED FROM PAGE 124

- At this point you have to knead in the cheddar cheese. It may seem like an impossible task, but eventually, it will all be distributed in the dough.
- Cut the dough ball in half. Let one wait, covered with the towel, while you cut the first into three even-sized strips. Roll these pieces into ropes, about a foot-long each. Pinch all three together at the top. Braid the three pieces together and pinch them together again at the bottom.
- Brush lightly with water and sprinkle with sesame seeds.
- Repeat with the second piece of dough.
- Lightly grease two jelly roll pans and lay one braid on each. Cover each with a tea towel.
- Let rise again until they are doubled in size.
- Heat oven to 375 F and bake loaves for about 25 minutes, or until nice and brown.
- Makes 2 medium loaves.

See photograph on page **129**

WINE FOR HARVEST SCRAMBLED EGGS: Egg dishes call for something with bubbles, like Kalala's Sparkling Gewürztraminer or See Ya Later Ranch Brut; or 8th Generation's frizzante style wines; or an effervescent apple cider from Sea Cider.

Harvest Scrambled Eggs

The eggs are so creamy they just barely hold the veggies together. It's a perfect filling to stuff into something like a crisp popover, and it looks appetizing with all the colours.

1/2 red pepper
1/2 green pepper
1 green onion
3 tbsp. (45 ml) cheddar
4 eggs
pinch of butter
1 c. (250 ml) chopped spinach
salt and pepper, to taste

- Mince fresh vegetables and grate cheese. Beat eggs and add all the ingredients except the spinach.
- Melt a pinch of butter in a non-stick pan and toss in the spinach. Stir for a second or two, then add egg mixture.
- Stir over medium heat for just a few minutes, until it's cooked, but still moist.
- Serves 2 to 4.

See photograph on page **130**

Parmesan Popovers with Rosemary

Light and crisp outside, creamy inside, these make great cases for creamed dishes like leftover chicken or ham, but they're also yummy for breakfast or brunch with a dollop of scrambled eggs in them.

oil spray, as needed
sprinkling of parmesan cheese
2 eggs
1 c. (250 ml) milk
1 tbsp. (15 ml) melted butter
1 tbsp. (15 ml) parmesan cheese
1/4 tsp. (1 ml) salt
1 c. (250 ml) flour
1/2 tsp. (2 ml) fresh rosemary

- Pre-heat oven to 425 F.
- Generously spray custard cups, popover tins or muffin tins with oil, sprinkling a little parmesan in as well.
- For best results, have ingredients at room temperature and pre-heat the tins.
- Beat eggs until light. Add milk and continue beating, then add melted butter.
- As you continue beating, add finely grated parmesan and salt, then flour and minced rosemary, beating until the mixture is creamy.
- Divide amongst 6-8 hot containers and bake for about 15 minutes on lowest rack in the oven.Don't open the oven, but turn the heat down to 350 F for a further 20 minutes or until they're nicely browned.
- Serves 2 to 4.

Little Apple Cakes

These special pancakes can be served for breakfast, brunch, a snack or dessert. Serve with bacon or ham, a sharp cheddar cheese, maple syrup or jam, topped with fresh fruit or just plain.

3/4 c. (175 ml) flour
1/4 c. (60 ml) oat bran
1 tbsp. (15 ml) sesame seeds
1 tsp. (5 ml) baking powder
1 tsp. (5 ml) cinnamon
1/2 tsp. (2 ml) salt
1/2 tsp. (2 ml) nutmeg
1/4 tsp. (1 ml) ginger
2 apples
2 eggs
1/2 c. (125 ml) milk
1 tbsp. (15 ml) maple syrup
2 tbsp. (30 ml) vegetable oil
icing sugar to garnish

- In a medium-sized bowl thoroughly mix dry ingredients, including seeds and spices.
- Core and chop apples. Peel if you wish.
- Beat eggs in a small bowl and add milk and maple syrup and combine.
- Heat half the oil in a large non-stick pan. Combine wet and dry ingredients.
- Drop by large spoonful on medium-hot pan and flip when browned on the first side. Remove to serving dish when nicely browned and puffed . Sprinkle with icing sugar.
- Repeat until all the batter is cooked.
- Serves 2-8, depending on how they're used.

See photographs for both on page 130

11. Dress Parties

HALLOWEEN HOWL

Halloween is not like it was in the old days: roaming the neighbourhood in the dark, yelling at adults for free sweets. Wow. What kid wouldn't want to move the goal posts like that?

Sure, when we were really young, adults were close by, just outside the flashlight's beam, but you could almost forget they were there – and anyway, they let you do all sorts of things you normally couldn't.

But, when we got a bit older, we had a taste of true freedom at Halloween, though there was an element of responsibility in it – you had to be home on time or there would be deep trouble.

But, you still got to roam around the neighbourhood dressed up as someone else – and that was pretty exciting.

Today most parents prefer to hold parties for youngsters where they can gather to be frightful.

It's the one day in the year they are encouraged to do all those things they usually aren't supposed to: dress in someone else's clothes, leer and otherwise make rude faces, eat too many sweets, demand treats and talk funny.

Who would deny them the one day when they can do all that instead of being good?

When it comes to Halloween food, let your little goblins help decorate, whether it's a personal meatloaf or a cookie.

Icebox or refrigerator cookies are very convenient because they don't all have to be baked at once. If the kids are helping, you can make the dough up well ahead of time, and then have them decorate when it's convenient.

Many adults never really outgrow the fun of Halloween, whether it's the costumes, pumpkin carving, spooky movies and music, scary pranks or just enjoying the treats that go with the day.

Just weeks after Halloween, there's a less scary sort of party around the television set or in the stadium, as football season's whistle blows and the annual Grey Cup is celebrated.

Nibblies are appreciated then, too.

When I have company I like recipes that can be made ahead of time. Ones where at least some of the work is done ahead, and only a little last-minute preparation is needed.

That way, I can join in the fun too.

Do remember, though, with the return to standard time, it gets darker earlier. If you have herbs still lingering in the garden, gather them early.

I once made a big pot of clam chowder and found myself prowling around in the rain, out in the dark, with a flashlight and a pair of scissors, groping for the thyme and parsley.

Luckily, when my garden is buried underneath a foot of snow, most produce shelves offer fresh herbs that some local farmer – with a greener thumb than mine – grows all winter. How fortunate!

Appetizer Beef Cubes

This is a simply delicious marinade for beef, and these little cubes are good for serving at Grey Cup because guys tend to like to chew on a chunk of beef. These are perfect dipped into the Curry Peanut Sauce (see index). The marinade would be great with cubes of chicken or pork too.

2 lb. (1 kg) beef steak

MARINADE:
2 tbsp. (30 ml) soy sauce
2 tbsp. (30 ml) brown sugar
1 tbsp.(15 ml) cornstarch
1 tbsp. (15 ml) fresh ginger, minced
1 tbsp. (15 ml) water

- Cube beef in bite-sized little pieces and put in a bowl.
- Combine all the marinade ingredients in that bowl and stir well with the meat. Marinate overnight.
- Toss into a drizzle of hot oil in a wok or deep frypan and stir-fry until browned and medium rare. Remove from the pan by skewering with a decorative cocktail pick of some sort, and arrange on a serving plate.
- You could also barbecue them on skewers or cook them under the broiler.
- Serve with the peanut dipping sauce.

See photograph on page **131**

Ghostly Meatloaves

These are mini meat loaves, so they cook more quickly than a large one, and they're lots of fun for kids to decorate with mashed potatoes and vegetables.

1 carrot
1 onion
1/2 c. (125 ml) oat bran
1 lb. (454 g) lean ground beef
1 egg
1/4 c. (60 ml) ketchup or chili sauce
1 tbsp. (15 ml) Worcestershire sauce
1/2 tsp. (2 ml) hot pepper sauce
1/4 tsp. (1 ml) salt
1/4 tsp. (1 ml) pepper

mashed potatoes, carrots, celery, peppers

- Pre-heat oven to 350 F.
- Grate carrot and mince onion.
- You could substitute bread or cracker crumbs for the oat bran, but the oat bran tastes better.
- Combine all ingredients and mix thoroughly.
- Spoon into muffin cups, or into paper cupcake liners in a muffin tin.
- Bake for about 20 to 25 minutes.
- Top with warm mashed potatoes, carrot or celery eyes, pepper mouth etc., or with a drizzle of salsa or tomato sauce.
- Makes a dozen.

See photograph on page **132**

WINE FOR GHOSTLY MEATLOAVES: *The trick is to serve wine that does not overshadow meat loaf. I prefer a sensibly-priced Merlot Cabernet blend from such producers as Gehringer Brothers, Prospect Winery and Sumac Ridge.*

TOP:
Grape & Wine Jelly with Jalapenos

Recipe on page 105

BOTTOM:
Braided Bread with Cheese & Onion

Recipe on page 124

TOP:
Harvest Scrambled Eggs
WITH
Parmesan Popovers with Rosemary

Recipes on pages **125 & 126**

BOTTOM:
Little Apple Cakes

Recipe on page **126**

TOP:
Appetizer Beef Cubes

Recipe on
page **128**

BOTTOM:
Witches' Fingers

Recipe on
page **133**

TOP:
Ghostly Meatloaves

Recipe on page **128**

BOTTOM:
Elise's Cheese Ball

Recipe on page **134**

Witch's Fingers

Be creative and ghoulish with these scary, but yummy, cookies. These would be great fun to make with your favourite youngsters, whether those are your own, your grandchildren, a friend's or the neighbours.

1 c. (250 ml) softened butter
1 c. (250 ml) icing sugar
1 egg
1 tsp. (5 ml) almond extract
1 tsp. (5 ml) vanilla
2 3/4 c. (675 ml) flour
1 tsp. (5 ml) baking powder
1 tsp. (5 ml) salt
3/4 c. (175 ml) blanched almonds
1 19-gram tube of red decorator gel

- In medium-sized bowl, beat together butter, sugar, egg, almond extract and vanilla. Whisk the flour, baking powder and salt, then stir into butter mixture.
- Cover and refrigerate for 30 minutes.
- Working with one quarter of the dough at a time, and keeping remaining dough refrigerated, roll a heaping teaspoonful into a finger shape between your hands.
- Press almond firmly into one end for the fingernail. Push it in rounded end first, so the point sticks out over the dough a bit.
- Press in centre to create knuckle shape. Using a paring knife, mark slashes in several places to form knuckle folds.
- Bake in 325 F. oven for 20 to 25 minutes or until golden brown.
- Let cool for five minutes.
- Lift up almond.
- Squeeze just a dab of red decorator gel onto nail bed and press almond back in place, so gel oozes out from underneath.
- Makes 24 to 30 fingers.

See photograph on page **131**

Elise's Cheese Ball

This is really good, and can be made a day or a week ahead to allow the flavours to mingle and mellow a bit. It can also be frozen or made fresh and served right away. This can be rolled in orange cheddar cheese and shaped like a pumpkin for Halloween or rolled in nuts and shaped like a football for a Grey Cup party or create a winter snowman with it.

8 oz. (227 g) cream cheese
6 oz. (170 g) sharp cheddar
2 tsp. (10 ml) sour cream
2 tsp. (10 ml) green onion
1/4 tsp. (1 ml) Worcestershire
cheese, nuts or minced herbs to garnish

- Soften cream cheese by letting it warm in a bowl or soften in the microwave for 30 seconds. Add the grated cheddar cheese, sour cream or yogurt, minced green onion (you could also add some minced green pepper and/or sweet pickles), and Worcestershire sauce.
- Mush everything together thoroughly and form it into a ball with your hands.
- Just before serving, roll the cheese ball in chopped almonds, walnuts or pecans; or in chopped fresh herbs such as parsley or chives. Chill.
- Serve with crackers.

See photograph on page **132**

Chicken Livers with Lemon

These are great as finger food or for a meal with a Greek salad.

1 lb. (.5 kg) chicken livers
flour, salt and pepper, for dredging
1 garlic clove
1 tbsp. (15 ml) oregano
1/2 c. (125 ml) sweet red onion
1/2 lemon
1 t bsp. (15 ml) olive oil
2 tsp. (10 ml) butter

- If serving as an appetizer, cut chicken livers into bite-sized pieces first.
- Dredge livers in flour, salt and pepper.
- Mince garlic and fresh oregano and chop onion. Zest half a lemon and mince the zest.
- Heat olive oil and melt butter over medium heat and brown chicken livers. Cook for about 20 minutes.
- Add oregano, garlic and lemon zest.
- Squeeze juice from lemon over top and serve garnished with raw sweet red onion.

See photograph on page **149**

Rumaki

This old favourite that likely originated in Hawaii, is familiar to many generations of Grey Cup partiers, I'm sure.

6 chicken livers
1/4 c. (60 ml) teriyaki sauce
6 water chestnuts
6 bacon slices

- Pre-heat oven to 425 F.
- Cut chicken livers into bite-sized pieces, probably in half.
- Marinate chicken livers in teriyaki sauce overnight, or for at least an hour.
- Cut water chestnuts in half, or into enough pieces to match the chicken livers.
- Half cook the bacon (in the microwave works well), making sure it's not crisp.
- Cut it the right lengths to wrap around one piece each of chicken liver and water chestnut.
- Wrap each little package and secure with a toothpick.
- Bake for about 10 minutes or until bacon is crisp.

WINE FOR RUMAKI:
You probably would not serve Icewine at a Grey Cup party. Even so, Riesling Icewine (Jackson-Triggs, Gehringer, Paradise Ranch) is an impressive apéritif with the savoury flavours of chicken liver.

Stuffed Cucumber Rollups

These are simple to make, look quite flashy and are fun. They taste pretty good too. The filling makes a good spread for crackers as well. With the red and green, they'd be pretty around Christmas too.

1/4 c. (60 ml) cream cheese
1 tbsp. (15 ml) sweet red pepper
1 tbsp. (15 ml) Asian sweet chili sauce
pinch of coarse salt
1/4 tsp. (1 ml) cracked black pepper
long English cucumber
fresh cilantro, chives or parsley
toothpicks

- Soften cream cheese and combine with finely-minced red pepper, chili sauce, sea salt and freshly cracked black pepper.
- Refrigerate until ready to make rollups.
- Use a peeler to slice long strips of cucumber with ribbons of green skin on either side. Use the first all-green slice for something else. About half the cucumber's length is suitable for one rollup.
- Lay the strips on your work area.
- Cut a pencil-thick strip of cream cheese about the same width as your cucumber and lay it at one end.
- Roll the strip of cucumber up around the cream cheese and secure the ends with a toothpick.
- Stand up on end to serve. Top each with a tiny sprig of fresh herb.
- Makes 2 doz. or so.

See photograph on page **149**

Curried Beef Packets

For Grey Cup, try forming these into football shapes, using whatever pastry strikes your fancy. For Christmas, perhaps you could wrap them up like a present or a scrunch up the top like a Santa sack. I used wonton wrappers last time and they were great. Baking times here are based on the pastry used. You can easily double the recipe.

FILLING:
1/2 c. (125 ml) onions
1 tbsp. (15 ml) minced ginger
1 garlic clove
1 stalk bok choy
drizzle of oil
1 tbsp. (15 ml) curry powder
1/4 lb. (112 g) ground beef
1 tbsp. (15 ml) chutney
1/4 tsp. (1 ml) salt

pastry such as wonton wrappers/
    phyllo

- Finely chop onions, ginger, garlic and bok choy (You could substitute celery).
- In a medium frypan with a drizzle of oil over medium heat, soften onions and ginger, then add minced garlic and stir in the curry powder, letting it cook for a minute.
- Next, push the vegetables to the side and add the lean ground beef. Stir a bit while it browns. Add the bok choy or celery and cook for another couple of minutes.
- Add remaining ingredients and mix thoroughly. Cool.
- If using wonton wrappers, place a teaspoon of filling at one end and roll up, folding in the sides as you go. Put a drop of water on the remaining wrapper end to seal. Set on a pan, seam side down.
- Bake at 400 F for about 15 minutes.
- Makes about two dozen little rolls.

See photograph on page **150**

WINE FOR
CURRIED BEEF
PACKETS:
It's a Grey Cup party! Serve beer.

Pig in a Pod with Apples

This is a whole meal stuffed into an acorn or other small winter squash, and it's just delicious.

2 acorn squash
1/2 lb. (250 g) ground pork
pat of butter
1 onion
1 c. (250 ml) cabbage
1 apple
1 knob ginger
2 tsp. (10 ml) fresh thyme
1 tbsp. (15 ml) fresh sage
1/2 tsp. (2 ml) cayenne
salt and pepper to taste

WINE FOR PIG IN A POD WITH APPLES: *This has Ehrenfelser written all over it. CedarCreek releases a killer Ehrenfelser each spring and you need to stock up if you want some for dinners in the fall. Other good producers of this peachy white are Summerhill, Gray Monk and Gehringer Brothers.*

- Pre-heat oven to 400F
- Cut the squash in half and scoop out the seeds and membranes, leaving the meat and shell intact.
- Set face down in a roasting pan with just a half-inch of water and bake for about 20 minutes while you prepare the filling.
- Cook ground pork or sausage meat in a deep frypan or wok until all pink is gone, draining off any excess fat. Remove the pork.
- Add butter or oil to pan and fry a large chopped onion, shredded, chopped cabbage, cored chopped apple and a spoonful of minced ginger, cooking until the onion and cabbage are just limp.
- Season with fresh herbs, salt and peppers and return pork to pan, mixing well.
- Remove squash from oven and turn over, cut side up. Fill each with the pork and cabbage mixture.
- Return to the oven for a further half hour.
- Serves 4.

See photograph on page **150**

Butternut Squash Soup with Prawns

With or without the prawns this soup is tummy-filling and warming. It makes a great vegetarian meal, if you substitute vegetable broth for the chicken. You can just leave the brandy out, but it takes this to another level in flavour.

1 large onion
2 garlic cloves
1 tbsp. (15 ml) fresh ginger
2 small butternut squashes
2 large carrots
drizzle of olive oil
1 tbsp. whole cumin seeds
3 c. (750 ml) chicken stock
salt and pepper
1 tbsp. (15 ml) fresh chives
1/2 c. (125 ml) light cream
poached prawns
brandy

- Chop onion and mince garlic and ginger.
- Peel and chop squashes into one-inch dice (two cups or so), and slice carrots.
- Drizzle a little olive oil into a large pot and heat the cumin seeds over medium heat. Add the minced fresh ginger and the onions.
- When they're soft add the garlic, squash and carrots. Cook for a minute or two.
- Add chicken stock, bring to bubbling, and turn down to a simmer, cover with a lid. Simmer for 20 to 30 minutes, stirring occasionally.
- Crush vegetables with a potato masher, or use a blender for a finer texture. Taste and season.
- Mince fresh chives and add them with the light cream, heating just until warmed through.
- Serve garnished with poached prawns and a drizzle of brandy in each bowl.
- Serves 4-6.

See photograph on page **151**

WINE FOR BUTTERNUT SQUASH SOUP WITH PRAWNS: *I would like one of those tasty white blends that everyone seems to be releasing, like Hatfield's Fuse or Mixed Blessings from Blasted Church or White Meritage from Sumac Ridge or Jackson-Triggs.*

Gord's Caribbean Pumpkin Soup

My version of this delectable spicy soup was almost like a stew, and a bowl constituted a very filling, but very satisfying meal. Just add a biscuit on the side. It's great for using up bits of leftover ham.

WINE FOR GORD'S CARIBBEAN PUMPKIN SOUP: *A refreshing partner would be a rosé like Poplar Grove's Monster Rosé or 8th Generation's Pinot Meunier Rosé.*

1 onion
1 carrot
4 paste (plum) tomatoes
1 tbsp. (15 ml) butter
2 sprigs thyme
1 tsp. (5 ml) summer savoury
1/2 tsp. (2 ml) paprika
1/2 tsp. (2 ml) salt
1/2 tsp. (2 ml) garlic powder
1/4 tsp. (1 ml) black pepper
1/4 tsp. (1 ml) cayenne pepper
1/4 tsp. (1 ml) dried oregano
1 tbsp. (15 ml) flour
4 c. (1 l) chicken stock
4 c. (1 l) pumpkin
1 c. (250 ml) ham cubes

- Chop onion, carrot and tomatoes (I use frozen ones from my garden), and saute in a big pot in a spoonful of butter.
- Add seasonings. When it's all nicely mixed and the onion's soft, add flour and mix well.
- Gradually stir in warm chicken stock, bring just to bubbling, then cover and simmer for 45 minutes.
- Add pumpkin.
- (I roasted a medium-sized pumpkin, cut in half, in the oven for about an hour, then scooped out the pulp from one half and smashed it up. If you pureed it the soup's texture would be different. Either way's probably fine.)
- Add minced ham.
- Simmer for 15 minutes more, then taste for salt and pepper and add if needed.
- Delicious the second day, too.
- Serves 4-6.

Pumpkin Date Cookies

Make these with your own pumpkin, which you've roasted in the oven until soft, or buy a tin of it. Guess which tastes best.

1/2 c. (125 ml) butter
1 c. (250 ml) brown sugar
1 egg
1 c. (250 ml) pumpkin
1 tsp. (5 ml) vanilla
3/4 c. (175 ml) white flour
1/2 c. (125 ml) whole wheat flour
1/2 c. (125 ml) oatmeal
1/2 tsp. (3 ml) baking soda
1 tsp. (5 ml) cinnamon
1 tsp. (5 ml) ginger
1/2 tsp. (3 ml) allspice
1/4 tsp. (1 ml) nutmeg
1/4 tsp. (1 ml) salt
1/2 c. (125 ml) chopped dates

- Pre-heat oven to 375F.
- Cream butter and add brown sugar.
- Beat well, then add egg, pumpkin and vanilla and combine thoroughly.
- In separate bowl mix dry ingredients except dates, then fold them with the creamed ingredients.
- Add dates and drop by spoonful onto a greased cookie sheet.
- Bake for about 12 minutes.
- Cool on a wire rack.

Mom's Pumpkin Loaf

Pumpkins are good for way more than just Jack-O-Lanterns. They make muffins and loaves nutritious, moist and delicious.

1 1/2 c. (375 ml) flour
1 tsp. (5 ml) baking powder
1/2 tsp. (2 ml) baking soda
1/4 tsp. (1 ml) salt
1 tsp. (5 ml) cinnamon
1/2 c. (125 ml) white sugar
1/2 c. (125 ml) brown sugar
1 c. (250 ml) raisins
2 eggs
1/2 c. (125 ml) oil
1 c. (250 ml) pumpkin

- Pre-heat oven to 350F.
- Combine dry ingredients and raisins in a large bowl.
- Beat eggs with oil and pumpkin.
- Combine wet and dry ingredients until just moistened, then pour into a greased loaf pan.
- Bake for 50 to 60 minutes or until a skewer comes out clean when inserted in the middle.
- Cool on a rack, then turn out, or slice in the pan.

Icebox Spice Cookies

These taste warm and mellow, perfect for nippy fall and winter days. You could keep the well-wrapped dough in the freezer or fridge until the grandkids come over, then liberate the roll, slice them up and present fresh-from-the-oven cookies to your favourite people.

1 c. (250 ml) butter
1 c. (250 ml) brown sugar
1/2 tsp. (3 ml) baking soda
1/4 tsp. (1 ml) salt
1/2 tsp. (3 ml) ground cardamom
1/2 tsp. (3 ml) cinnamon
1/2 tsp. (3 ml) ground ginger
1/4 tsp. (1 ml) nutmeg
1/8 tsp. (.5 ml) cloves
1 egg
1 tsp. (5 ml) vanilla
1 1/2 c. (375 ml) white flour
1 c. (250 ml) whole wheat flour

- Pre-heat oven to 375 F.
- Beat butter (not soft margarine), then add sugar, baking soda and spices. Add egg and vanilla and beat until thoroughly creamed.
- Add flour gradually and beat for as long as you can use the electric mixer, then use a spoon to add the remainder.
- Shape into two cookie-sized rolls and wrap in wax paper.
- Chill until easy to handle, an hour or so, then cut into 1/8-inch slices.
- Bake on an ungreased cookie sheet at 375F for about 10 minutes.
- Cool on a wire rack.
- Let children create faces on them, using a snip of dried fruit and a couple of chocolate chips, or you can roll them in chopped nuts before slicing into cookies.
- If you keep a roll in the freezer, thaw in the fridge before making cookies. A roll can be kept in the refrigerator for several days.

12. Comfort Food

A RETURN TO OUR ROOTS

In fall, shorter days, frosty mornings and colder nights make us want to draw the drapes and light the fire.

With doors and windows firmly closed against inclement weather, the aromas from your cook stove become a focal point for the family.

Meals that go together in one pot, roasting pan, or dish are top attractions for busy days, but on the weekend, be prepared to try something a bit more challenging.

Food with flavour and nutrition is important, as is the use of fresh, locally-grown B.C. ingredients, wherever possible.

Presentation, including contrasting colors and an inviting appearance are irresistible. Don't hesitate to add a sprig of fresh parsley or any other herb you have available to the serving dish. Even freshly-dried herbs, crumbled and sprinkled on a serving dish can make all the difference in presentation.

Contrasting colours on the plate are much more appetizing than a monochrome. They're also indicative of the range of vitamins tastily tucked into the food on your plate, so satisfy nutritional needs, pamper the body and the palate in one fell swoop.

Buttered crumbs are a good garnish for something as simple as steamed broccoli or cauliflower, as is a grating of cheese.

Comfort foods are ones that taste good when you need a little cuddle – perhaps on a nippy autumn evening, or a snowy winter night after a day outdoors.

Soups generally fall within that category, and so do casseroles and stews.

They're quite often foods your grandma, mom or your favorite aunt used to make when you were a kid, and the smell of them cooking brings back memories of endess love, security with no worries, and more fun around the next corner.

In our more-mature days of nothing but bills around the next corner, that's a nice feeling to re-capture, even if it's only for a moment or an evening.

There is a trend toward returning to our roots; to reducing the clutter of sophistication and technology to find pleasure in simpler things.

That trend is particularly apparent in our food where such traditional basics as a pan of freshly roasted root vegetables is again considered a treat to accompany a joint of meat or a bird.

We're digging out mother's or granny's old cookbook and leafing through the spattered pages for gems of recipes we have vague memories of enjoying when we were kids.

Sometimes those memories have become indistinct with time but the feeling is unmistakeable when we're able to successfully resurrect the smells or flavours which are attached to rosy childhood memories.

Roasted Harvest Roots

Browning earthy roots in a hot oven turns them all into sweet delicacies that are crisp outside and soft inside. Fresh herbs add the crowning touch. The quantities of vegetables, and the combination you decide to use, depends on your taste and what's available from the garden or produce store.

1 onion
1 potato
2 parsnips
2 carrots
2 yams
2 summer squash
1 tbsp. (15 ml) olive oil
2 tsp. (10 ml) fresh lemon thyme
2 tsp. (10 ml) rosemary
fresh ground pepper and salt, to taste

- Pre-heat oven to 400 F.
- We love onions, so I'd use a large one, along with a large potato, or two small ones, for instance.
- Cut onions into six to eight wedges and dice root vegetables into chunks roughly an inch or two square.
- Toss into a deep bowl with olive oil, lemon thyme (substitute thyme and lemon balm or lemon zest) and fresh or dried chopped rosemary. Once all the vegetables are coated with a thin film of oil, sprinkle with freshly ground black pepper and a bit of coarse sea salt.
- Pour into a roasting pan and bake for about half an hour, or until browned.
- If you have summer squash available they make a nice contrast in colour, but they must be added only in the last 10 minutes or so of cooking or they turn to mush.
- Cut green zucchini into thick diagonal slices, and wedge a yellow scallop squash.
- Toss as with the root vegetables in a deep bowl with a drizzle of olive oil and fresh herbs, salt and pepper, then add to roasting pan.
- Serve garnished with a sprinkle of fresh, chopped herbs such as rosemary, parsley, thyme or chives.
- Serves 3-5.

French Onion Soup

This is delicious just as it is, or it can make a grand entrance, served over dried or toasted French bread, sprinkled with Swiss cheese and run under the broiler until it browns and bubbles.

2 lb. (1 kg) onions
2 tbsp. (30 ml) butter
2 tbsp. (30 ml) oil
1 tsp. (5 ml) salt
1/4 c. (60 ml) flour
2 qt. (2 l) stock
1/4 c. (60 ml) dry sherry/opt.

- Cut onions in half lengthwise, then slice them putting the flat side down to make slicing easier. Melt butter in a large, heavy soup or stew pot, add your choice of cooking oil, and when it's hot, throw in all the onions.
- Sprinkle salt over it all, and stir together.
- Cook the onions over low heat, uncovered, for half an hour or so, stirring occasionally to make sure none brown. They should be limp and translucent.
- While the onions are cooking, heat about five cups (1.25 l) of beef stock and three cups (750 ml) of chicken stock, ready to add to the cooked onions.
- Sprinkle flour over the onions and stir it in, cooking it for a few minutes.
- Add hot stock mixture to onions, increasing the heat and stirring until it all returns to bubbling.
- Simmer, partly covered, for another half hour or more, stirring occasionally.
- Taste for seasoning and add salt and pepper and a healthy dash of dry sherry, if desired.

See photograph on page **151**

WINE FOR FRENCH ONION SOUP: *Venturi-Schulze makes an exceptional off-dry wine called Brandenburg #3, the flavours of which are concentrated by simmering. A glass of that would take this onion soup to a whole new experience.*

Emily's Wonton Soup

This is a bit fussy to make, but it's a complete meal and quite tasty.

purchased wonton wrappers

FILLING:
1/2 lb. (200 g) ground beef, pork or chicken
1 tbsp. (15 ml) soy sauce
2 tsp. (10 ml) cornstarch
1/4 tsp. (1 ml) salt
2 drops sesame oil
a dash of pepper

BROTH:
3-4 stems of bok choy
2 green onions, to garnish
6 c. (2 l) chicken or beef broth
3 tbsp. (45 ml) soy sauce
2-5 drops sesame oil
salt and pepper, to taste

WINE FOR EMILY'S WONTON SOUP:
I would prefer the crisp and tangy flavours of apple wine or apple cider with this. Raven Ridge in Kelowna makes both dry apple wine and richly-flavoured iced apple ciders that will turn this into a grand event.

- To form the wontons combine meat, soy sauce, cornstarch, salt, sesame oil and pepper in a bowl. Lay out wonton skins and wet with your finger, two sides lf the wrapper in an 'L' shape. Drop a teaspoon-sized ball of the meat mixture into the middle.
- Fold one corner of the wonton skin diagonally to the other corner and press the edges together. The moisture should help them stick together.
- Wet each pointed end, grab the flappy end from the top and flip upward. Push the two wetted ends together.

BROTH:
- Slice bok choy into thin strips, across the stem. Sliver green onions on the diagonal and set aside.
- Mix broth, soy sauce, sesame oil, salt and pepper. Let simmer over low heat for a few minutes until the wontons are ready and then bring it to a boil.
- Drop wontons into the broth and add bok choy. Let simmer for 10 to 15 minutes.
- Garnish with slivers of green onion.

Mom's Clam Chowder

This is the white style of clam chowder, without tomatoes, and it's pretty darn good.

1 large onion
4 slices bacon
1/2 green pepper
1 carrot
14-oz. (398 ml) clam nectar
4 c. (1 l) stock
2 med. potatoes
14 oz. (398 ml) clams, drained
1 c. (250 ml) 10 % cream
1/4 tsp. (1 ml) fresh thyme
1/4 tsp. (1 ml) paprika
1 tbsp. (15 ml) fresh parsley

- Saute the chopped onion and diced bacon in a large, heavy pot over medium heat until the onion is soft and the bacon cooked, keeping the pot covered.
- Finely chop the green pepper (it may be omitted) and carrot. Add to the pot and cook for a few minutes, stirring everything together.
- Pour in clam nectar and hot stock, either chicken or fish, and bring to a boil for five minutes.
- Lower heat and add potatoes which have been cut into 1/2-inch dice. (You may substitute 1/2 c. raw rice.)
- Simmer for 15 minutes with the lid on.
- Add drained, canned clams, whole scrubbed live clams, or a combination of the two, and the cream (you may substitute skim milk, but it won't be as rich), and simmer for five minutes more.
- Add salt and pepper to taste, then thyme, paprika and parsley just before serving.

Seafood Chowder with Dill

This is quick and simple to make and tastes fantastic the first time – and it's good heated up as well.

3 slices of bacon
1 large onion
3 carrots
3 celery stalks
2 c. (500 ml) one per cent milk
1 c. (250 ml) 10 per cent cream
1 large potato, grated
1/4 lb. (100 g) salmon
1/4 lb. (100 g) red snapper or cod
1/4 lb. (100 g) scallops
1/4 lb. (100 g) prawns
1/2 c. (125 ml) dry white wine
1 c. (250 ml) fresh dill
sea salt and freshly-ground black
   pepper

WINE FOR SEAFOOD CHOWDER WITH DILL:
Chowders ask for crisp whites with good acidity. I would recommend a Riesling from, for example, 8th Generation or Jackson-Triggs or Nk'Mip Cellars or Hester Creek's Trebbiano.

- Chop bacon and brown in a large pot over medium heat, then pour off any excess fat.
- Chop onion, thinly slice carrots and slice celery. Add onion to pot with bacon and stir, cooking until it begins to soften.
- Add carrots and stir for a few minutes, then celery.
- When softened, add milk and cream and stir well.
- Grate a scrubbed potato and add to the pot. Bring the mix to bubbling, stirring regularly, cooking for a few minutes to soften the potato and thicken the chowder.
- Chop the seafood into bite-sized pieces and add to the mix with the wine.
- Bring back to bubbling and stir. Lower heat, cover and let cook for about five minutes.
- Chop fresh dill and stir in.
- Taste for seasoning and serve.
- Serve 4.

See photograph on page **152**

Chicken with Ginger & Orange Sauce

This is a great favourite with our family. We usually serve it with long grain brown rice, and a green vegetable like beans or broccoli.

10 chicken thighs
1 onion
1 tbsp. (15 ml) fresh ginger
1 orange, zested
3/4 c. (175 ml) orange juice
1/4 c. (60 ml) soy sauce
2 tbsp. (30 ml) honey
1 tbsp. (15 ml) cornstarch
1 tbsp. (15 ml) cold water
salt and pepper, to taste

- Skin chicken. Dice onion. Mince fresh ginger. Zest orange and mince the zest. Squeeze orange juice into a bowl and add measured orange juice, soy and honey and combine well.
- Blend cornstarch and cold water in a tiny bowl and set aside.
- Drizzle a little oil in a Dutch oven over medium-high heat and soften onion chunks.
- Add minced ginger and stir, then brown chicken parts.
- Pour orange juice mixture over it all and bring to bubbling.
- Simmer and cover, cooking for about 45 minutes or until chicken is tender.
- Remove chicken parts to a serving dish.
- Bring the sauce to bubbling and blend the cornstarch mixture in. Stir until it's clear and it thickens.
- Pour over chicken or return pieces to sauce.
- Serves 4-5.

WINE FOR CHICKEN WITH GINGER & ORANGE SAUCE:
Ginger and wine can be a tough match but the flavours here are subtle. Perhaps a glass of Auxerrois from one of the few producers still offering this tasty white – Gray Monk, Gehringer Brothers, Little Straw.

TOP:
Chicken Livers with Lemon

Recipe on page **134**

BOTTOM:
Stuffed Cucumber Roll-ups

Recipe on page **135**

TOP:
Curried Beef Packets

Recipe on page **136**

BOTTOM:
Pig in a Pod with Apples

Recipe on page **137**

TOP:
Butternut Squash Soup with Prawns
Recipe on page **138**

BOTTOM:
French Onion Soup
Recipe on page **144**

TOP:
**Seafood
Chowder
with Dill**

Recipe on
page **147**

BOTTOM:
**Den's
Italian
Meatballs**

WITH
**Den's
Spaghetti
Sauce**

Recipes on
pages **153 & 154**

Lemon & Garlic Chicken Casserole

Mediterranean flavours, but a quick and inexpensive meal in one dish, this would also stand up to a special occasion.

2 lb. (1 kg) chicken pieces
4 garlic cloves
1 lemon
2 tbsp. (30 ml) olive oil
2 tbsp. (30 ml) fresh oregano
2 tsp. (10 ml) fresh thyme
salt and pepper, to taste
4 potatoes
4 carrots
2 onions
1/4 c. (60 ml) dry wine

- Skin chicken pieces. Marinate for just a few minutes or overnight in the mixture of minced garlic, lemon juice and zest, olive oil, minced fresh herbs, or half the amount of dried, salt and pepper. I use the same large, flattish casserole dish I'll cook it all in.
- Pre-heat oven to 350 F.
- Scrub spuds and carrots. Quarter small potatoes, or cut larger ones into more chunks and slice carrots into half-inch chunks. Cut onions into wedges.
- Combine vegetables with the chicken and marinade, then drizzle a little dry wine, red or white, over it all, cover it and roast for one hour.
- Uncover and either turn the oven heat up or switch on the broiler for a few minutes to brown the potatoes.
- Serves 3-4.

WINE FOR LEMON & GARLIC CHICKEN CASSEROLE: *Serve whatever wine you cook with, always remembering that poor wine is never suitable for cooking. A full-flavoured Chardonnay, if white is used in cooking, and a Pinot Noir if red.*

Den's Italian Meatballs

He is Italian, so maybe that's why these are so good. Bake them instead of frying them: less fat and less mess.

1 garlic clove
1 tbsp. (15 ml) fresh oregano
2 tbsp. (30 ml) parmesan cheese
1 lb. (454 g) lean ground beef
1 egg
1/4 c. (60 ml) oat bran
1/4 c. (60 ml) ketchup
10 drops tobasco
1/2 tsp. (2 ml) Worcestershire sauce
1/4 tsp. (1 ml) salt
1/4 tsp. (1 ml) pepper

- Pre-heat oven to 350 F.
- Mince garlic and oregano, grate parmesan and combine all ingredients in a bowl. (You may substitute bread crumbs for the oat bran.)
- Roll into meatballs or just use a spoon to dab spoonfuls onto a baking sheet.
- Bake for 20 minutes.
- Makes 2-3 dozen.

See photograph on page **152**

Den's Spaghetti Sauce

You can make substitutions of amounts in this recipe to suit your taste, but this version is great.

1 large onion
1/2 green pepper
1 large garlic clove
2 tbsp. (30 ml) fresh oregano
drizzle of olive oil
8 whole mushrooms
14 oz. (398 ml) tin of tomatoes
14 oz. (398 ml) tin of tomato sauce
salt and pepper, to taste

- Chop onion and sweet pepper and mince garlic and fresh oregano (Substitute half the amount of dried, if necessary).
- Soften onion in a pot over medium heat in a drizzle of olive oil.
- Add minced garlic and mushrooms and cook for a minute or two.
- Add tomatoes and tomato sauce and bring to bubbling.
- Add green pepper and oregano.
- Turn the heat down to a simmer and cook for an hour or so.
- Season to taste.
- Serves 3-4.

See photograph on page **152**

Fruit Crisp

This is a classic dessert that even the youngsters could prepare, and it could be cooked either in the microwave or a regular oven. Pop it in after the roast has been removed, and it'll be done when everyone's finished the main course.

1 c. (250 ml) brown sugar
1/2 c. (125 ml) flour
1/2 c. (125 ml) oats
1 tsp. (5 ml) cinnamon
1/2 tsp. (2 ml) nutmeg
1/4 c. (60 ml) butter
6 c. (1.5 l) apples

- Combine sugar, flour, oats, and spices in a bowl and cut in butter until it's crumby.
- Butter a round deep 8-inch microwave-safe dish such as a casserole, or use a cake pan in the regular oven.
- Peel, core and slice apples into the dish. Drizzle with a bit of apple juice if they're not nice and juicy.
- Sprinkle sugar and flour topping over the apples.
- Bake for about 15 minutes on high in the microwave or a half-hour in a 350F oven.

See photograph on page **185**

WINE FOR DEN'S SPAGHETTI SAUCE: *Spaghetti and meatballs need a full-bodied but unpretentious red because you won't have time to swirl the wine while also swirling the spaghetti. Try a glass of Road 13's Honest John's Red or, for a real Italian experience, D'Angelo's Sette Copa.*

Beef Stroganoff with Veggies

This smooth, flavorful sauce with strips of lean beef is rich and creamy. A wide noodle such as fettucine is delicious with this dish, or boil up some little potatoes to serve under it. Leftovers are even better.

WINE FOR BEEF STROGANOFF WITH VEGGIES: *I would recommend a sturdy Burgundy-style red, like Desert Hills Gamay Noir, or a sturdy Bordeaux-style red, like Pétales d'Osoyoos from Osoyoos LaRose.*

1 onion
1/2 lb. (227 g) mushrooms
2 cloves of garlic
drizzle of oil
2 lb. (1 kg) lean beef
1/4 c. (60 ml) whole wheat flour
1/2 tsp. (2 ml) salt
1/4 tsp. (1 ml) pepper
drizzle of oil & a pat of butter
10 oz. (300 ml) of so of beef broth
1 tbsp. (15 ml) Worcestershire
1 stalk celery, chopped
carrots, to taste, sliced
1/2 c. (125 ml) plain yogurt or sour cream
1/4 c. (60 ml) dry white wine

- Slice onion and mushrooms and mince garlic.
- Heat oil in a deep frypan or Dutch oven, and saute sliced onions and mushrooms until the onions are limp. Add minced garlic.
- Meanwhile, drench strips of lean beef, perhaps from a round steak or roast, in flour seasoned with salt and pepper.
- Remove mushroom mixture and set aside.
- Add a drizzle of olive oil and a pat of butter to the pan and brown the beef strips. Remove from pan.
- Add beef broth, tinned or home made, and Worcestershire sauce, along with chopped vegetables.
- Stir and bring to bubbling, then return the meat to the pot; turn the heat down and simmer slowly until the meat is tender, a couple of hours if using a less tender cut of beef.
- You may cook it on the lowest heat on top of the stove or put it into a 350 F oven.
- Finish by adding yogurt or sour cream and wine and warm it through.
- Serve, sprinkled with fresh herbs, if available.
- Serves 8.

Winter

13. Entertaining Eats

COOKING WITH THE KIDS

Clear the decks, but don't clean the kitchen yet.

It's time to begin making some goodies for the holiday season.

I know a very well-organized grandma who loves to cook just as she loves each of those little (and big) grandchildren. At Christmas she combines those loves of cooking and family in the hope she can pass them on to those young ones.

One weekend in December she gathers together as many of the grandchildren as possible for a great big kitchen session at which everyone gets to put a finger in the pie – or the cookie dough.

It really doesn't matter much what goodies emerge from these sessions because they always make warm memories for everyone to carry home with them.

What a good family tradition to adopt.

We lived simply when my kids were little and they didn't have any of the colourful play dough most youngsters have today.

Instead, they had bread dough, cookie dough, biscuit dough and pastry dough.

I had a wonderful wood cookstove in our log home because no powerlines reached into our corner of the Cariboo, so I made almost everything from scratch.

And, the kids "helped."

With my trusty butcher block in the middle of the kitchen and that stove pumping out the heat, we'd have a ball while the snow drifted down outside the windows and the moose nibbled on willow twigs in the back yard.

The kids would be up to their elbows in flour and I probably had a few smears of it here and there as well. They'd knead their lumps of dough and form them while I worked on a larger one beside them.

We got some interesting shapes of bread, biscuits and cookies out of those sessions, but they had fun, and so did I.

Kids can learn a lot by helping out in the kitchen. The lessons range from chemistry to art; from the exercise of small muscles and coordination, to teamwork and following directions.

Along the road, it's a companionable way to achieve a satisfying result: something good that you can eat.

A session in the kitchen with the kids can be fun for everyone involved, except perhaps the clean-up crew.

Jimmy's Sugar Cookies

He probably doesn't have time to make his sugar cookies any more, but when he was little he loved to. Jimmy's now Jim and all grown up with facial hair, muscles and a family of his own, but he probably still has the memories hidden away somewhere.

2/3 c. (150 ml) butter
3/4 c. (175 ml) sugar
1 tsp. (5 ml) vanilla
1 egg
4 tsp. (20 ml) milk
2 c. (500 ml) flour
1 1/2 tsp. (8 ml) baking powder
1/4 tsp. (1 ml) salt

- Pre-heat oven to 375 F.
- Thoroughly cream the butter; sugar and vanilla with the beater. Add egg and beat until light and fluffy. Stir in milk. Whisk together flour, baking powder and salt, then blend into creamed mixture.
- Divide dough in half and chill for an hour so it's easier to work with.
- On lightly floured surface, roll out half the dough to about an eighth-inch thickness, leaving the other half in the refrigerator.
- Use cookie cutters or a cup or glass to cut out the shapes you'd like, then decorate or bake plain and ice later.
- Bake for about six to eight minutes. Cool slightly before removing to a rack.
- Makes about 24 cookies.

Mom's Maid of Honour Tarts

Mom always made these English delicacies, particularly around Christmas. I love the smell of them, and as a child, I loved the secret red spot of raspberry jam in the centre.

3 tbsp. (45 ml) butter
1 c. (250 ml) rice flour
1 c. (250 ml) sugar
2 eggs
1 tsp. (5 ml) almond flavourings
raspberry jam
18 tart shells

- Pre-heat oven to 375F.
- Melt butter and combine with all remaining ingredients except jam and tart shells.
- Place a dab of raspberry jam in the middle of each tart shell before spooning in the filling mixture.
- Bake for about 15 to 20 minutes, watching carefully to make sure they don't burn.
- They can be made ahead of time and frozen.

Pat's Gingerbread

Gingerbread people are an important part of growing up. The kids used to make one for each of their favorite people, decorate it and ice their name on it as a special Christmas gift.

1 c. (250 ml) butter
1 c. (250 ml) sugar
1/2 tsp. (2 ml) salt
1 egg
1 c. (250 ml) molasses
2 tbsp. (15 ml) vinegar
5 c. (750 ml) sifted flour
1 1/2 tsp. (8 ml) baking soda
1 tbsp. (15 ml) ginger
1 tsp. (5 ml) cinnamon
1 tsp. (5 ml) cloves

- Cream butter, sugar and salt; then beat in egg, molasses and vinegar.
- Combine dry ingredients with a whisk. Add dry ingredients to egg mixture and stir well.
- Refrigerate for a half-hour.
- Flour surface and rolling pin and roll out half the dough to desired thickness Keep the other half well-chilled.
- Grease cookie sheets, and pre-heat oven to 375F.
- Use gingerbread people cookie cutters to cut out your dough, place each carefully on the cookie sheet.
- Some decorations may be added before baking (round colourful candy-covered chocolates make great vest buttons), or ice them when baked and cooled.
- Bake for about six minutes and cool slightly before removing from cookie sheet.
- The number depends on your cookie cutters and ingenuity.

See photograph on page **185**

Fudgie Brownies

This recipe, or one very like it, has come to me from more than one source, but I got it first from my Mom. It's simple and very chocolatey.

2 tbsp. (30 ml) cocoa
3/4 c. (175 ml) dark brown sugar
1/2 c. (125 ml) butter
2 eggs
1/2 c. (125 ml) flour
1/4 tsp. (1 ml) salt
1/2 tsp. (2 ml) vanilla
1/2 c. (125 ml) walnuts

- Pre-heat oven to 325F.
- Combine cocoa and dark brown sugar.
- Melt butter and add, along with two large eggs, slightly beaten.
- Whisk flour and salt together, then mix into batter with vanilla.
- Add walnuts or chocolate chips if desired.
- Pour into greased 8x8x2-inch pan.
- Bake for 25 minutes, cool and cut into squares.

Mom's Fish Spread

This is very tasty served on crackers or cocktail rye bread slices. It can be made a month ahead and frozen.

4 oz. (120 g) tuna
2-7.5 oz. (212 g) tins sardines
3 tbsp. (45 ml) ketchup
1 tbsp. (15 ml) lemon juice
1 tbsp. (15 ml) Worcestershire
15 drops hot sauce

- Drain a tin of water-packed tuna and two tins of sardines and dump them into a flat-ish bowl where you can easily smush everything together with a fork.
- Add the remaining ingredients and thoroughly mix everything together. Test and alter the ingredients to your taste.

Potted Cheese

This is definitely not diet food. As the name implies this is probably of British origin, as my Mom was. Don't even think about fat or cholesterol, just enjoy a smear on a cracker and don't overdo it. It should be made a week or so ahead for the flavours to get happy together.

1/2 lb. (225 g) butter
1 lb. (454 g) aged cheddar
1/4 c. (60 ml) brandy
1 tbsp. (15 ml) Worcestershire
dash hot sauce

- Soften the butter and grate the well-aged cheddar cheese.
- Blend the two, then add the brandy and seasonings and work it into the butter and cheddar mix.
- For a different flavor you could substitute sherry, wine or beer for the brandy.
- This should be packed into small crocks, pots or jars and ripened at least 48 hours in the fridge before using.
- Makes a delightful gift.

Holiday Rum Balls

Decadently delicious, these improve after aging for a few weeks, but if keeping for longer than a month, freeze them for part of that time.

12 oz. (340 g) semi-sweet chocolate
1 c. (250 ml) sour cream
1/2 c. (125 ml) almond paste
pinch salt
1 1/2 c. (375 ml) butter
8 c. (2000 ml) vanilla wafers
2 c. (500 ml) pecans
3 c. (750 ml) icing sugar
2/3 c. (150 ml) cocoa
1 1/2 c. (375 ml) white rum
chocolate sprinkles, icing sugar or
    cocoa powder

- Melt chocolate and combine with sour cream, almond paste and salt. Cream thoroughly.
- Melt butter, crush wafers and chop pecans finely.
- In a large bowl combine wafer crumbs and the remaining ingredients except sprinkles. Mix until it begins to hold its shape.
- Add chocolate mixture and knead with your hands until it's well-blended and soft.
- Refrigerate until just firm enough to hold its shape, but soft enough to adhere to the sprinkles.
- Form spoonfuls into small balls, roll in the sprinkles, icing sugar or cocoa powder and set onto wax paper-covered trays to harden overnight in the refrigerator.
- Store in airtight containers and refrigerate. Remove from the fridge a few hours before serving to soften slightly.

WINE FOR HOLIDAY RUM BALLS:
After reading these cookie and tart recipes, I want a glass of port-style wine. Our wineries no longer call fortified wine Port, so you need to look for Calona's Sonata, Sumac Ridge's Pipe, Quails' Gate's Fortified Vintage Foch, Blasted Church's Amen, Alderlea's Hearth, Black Widow's Vintage One, La Frenz Tawny … and that is just part of the list.

Pork and Shrimp Pot Stickers

These are yummy little nibblies and putting them together would be a great family activity. Covered, they would keep very well over night in the refrigerator, already formed, ready to cook and serve hot. I used wonton wrappers and trimmed them into circles, but you can also purchase round pot sticker wrappers.

FILLING:
1 1/2 c. (375 ml) cabbage
1/4 lb. (113 g) shrimp or prawns
1 tbsp. (15 ml) minced ginger
1 garlic clove
1 green onion
1/4 lb. (113 g) lean ground pork
2 tsp. (10 ml) rice wine or sherry
1 tsp. (5 ml) soy sauce
1/8 tsp. (.5 ml) sesame oil
30 wrappers
1 beaten egg

- Mince raw cabbage, put in a sieve and pour a couple of cups of boiling water over it to wilt it. Use the cup to press out any extra moisture, then dump it into a medium-sized bowl.
- Mince shrimp or prawns, ginger, garlic and green onion, and add with remaining ingredients to cabbage and prawns. Mix well.
- Dot each wrapper with about two teasponfuls of filling and use your finger to paint the wrapper edge with beaten egg.
- Fold wrapper to envelope the filling and fold into little pleats all along the open edge, pressing firmly to form a little tightly-closed pouch full of the meat mixture.
- Set firmly on a plate, to flatten the bottom of the pouch.
- (These could be frozen in a single layer, covered with plastic wrap, for up to two weeks.)
- When you've completed enough to fill a large frypan with a lid, spray with a little oil or drizzle with a little olive oil and heat the pan to medium. Fill with pot stickers.
- When they've browned on the bottom, pour in enough water so it's about a quarter-inch deep in the bottom of the pan.
- Cover and turn the heat down to simmer them for 10 to 15 minutes.
- Serve with a dipping sauce on the side.
- You could use all pork or all shrimp instead of half and half.
- Makes 30.

DIPPING SAUCE:
2 tbsp. (30 ml) soy sauce
1 tbsp. (15 ml) dry sherry or rice wine
1/4 tsp. (1 ml) chilli powder
1/8 tsp. (.5 ml) sesame oil

- Combine and serve in individual little dipping dishes, or serve it in one bowl for everyone to share.

See photograph on page **186**

Curry Bites

These spicy tidbits have become a winter tradition in our family. They're delicious warm little bites on a blustery winter day. You could use any pastry, pie crust, puff or even crescent roll pastry in a tube. They can be made up and frozen individually before cooking and tossed into a freezer bag until needed.

FILLING:
2 green onions
12 water chestnuts
1/2 lb. (227 g) ground beef
3 tbsp. (45 ml) ketchup
2 tbsp. (30 ml) curry
2 tsp. (10 ml) sugar
1/2 tsp. (2 ml) salt

- Finely chop green onions and water chestnuts. Brown lean ground beef in a hot pan such as a wok.
- Add remaining ingredients and mix thoroughly. Cool.
- Pre-heat oven to 375 F. Roll out pastry and cut into small rectangles, about one inch by two inches; or two by three inches.
- Place one portion of filling on one side of each strip, then fold over and pinch the dough together, enclosing the little pockets of filling.
- Bake for 20 minutes until golden.
- OR: Freeze the little turnovers individually on cookie sheets, then toss the frozen bites into a big freezer bag until you want to use some.
- Place frozen turnovers on a greased cookie sheet and bake for 20-25 minutes in a 375-degree oven until they're golden brown.
- Makes 3 or 4 dozen.

Cheddar Pennies

Everyone gets hooked on these. There's lots of flavour packed in each crisp little bite.

1 c. (250 ml) flour
1/2 tsp. (2 ml) paprika
1/2 tsp. (2 ml) dry mustard
1/4 tsp. (1 ml) cayenne pepper
1/4 tsp. (1 ml) salt
1/2 c. (125 ml) butter
1 tsp. (5 ml) Worcestershire
3 c. (750 ml) cheddar cheese
hot pepper sauce
sesame or poppy seeds

- Combine dry ingredients and set aside.
- Cream softened butter, beating in Worcestershire sauce, then grated old, cheddar cheese.
- Thoroughly mix in dry ingredients, using your fingers at the end to shape into four rolls, about the diameter of a penny or a nickel.
- Wrap each in wax paper and refrigerate until firm.
- These will keep for several weeks in the refrigerator, ready to be sliced and baked as company comes in the door.
- To bake, pre-heat oven to 400 F.
- Slice roll into quarter-inch thick coins, placing each on a baking sheet, some distance apart.
- Add a drop of hot sauce to the top of each, smear it around, and top with sesame or poppy seeds. Press into the dough.
- Bake for eight to 10 minutes, or until crisp and golden brown.
- Each roll makes more than a dozen, depending on the thickness of your slices.

See photograph on page **186**

Little Cheese Puffs

I'm not sure about the origin of this recipe, but we've enjoyed it on special occasions for decades. It's jotted down on the back of an envelope, but I can't remember when I did that or where it came from.

1/2 c. (125 ml) water
2 1/2 tbsp. (38 ml) butter
1/2 c. (125 ml) flour
3 small eggs
3/4 c. (175 ml) cheddar
1/2 c. (125 ml) ham
1/8 tsp. (.5 ml) dry mustard
1 green onion

- In a heavy pot, bring water and butter to a boil.
- Remove from heat and add flour all at once, beating vigorously with a wooden spoon until blended.
- The mixture should thicken, leave the sides of the pot and form a ball.
- Beat in the eggs, one at a time, until the mixture is satiny smooth.
- Stir in cheese, ham, onion and dry mustard.
- Drop by teaspoon on greased cookie sheet and bake at 400 F for 10-15 minutes or until puffed and brown.

Mom's Rum Pudding

This wonderfully light, cold and creamy dessert is perfect after a heavy holiday meal.

1/2 c. (125 ml) white rum
1 tbsp. (15 ml) gelatin
3 eggs
1/2 c. (125 ml) sugar
1 c. (250 ml) whipping cream

- Heat rum in a small pot, but do not let it boil. Sprinkle on the gelatin powder and stir until it's completely dissolved.
- Pour into a large mixing bowl and let it cool to room temperature.
- Separate eggs, and in a small bowl beat egg yolks with a fork, then stir in white sugar until the mixture is creamy.
- Stir in cooled gelatine mixture.
- Beat egg whites until stiff but not dry and fold in egg and gelatin mixture.
- Finally, whip cream to soft peak stage and fold in carefully until completely incorporated.
- Transfer to serving dish, cover and chill for at least two hours.
- This is even better if it's made one day and served the next.
- Top with preserved, frozen or fresh fruit such as canned peaches, cherries or unsweetened strawberries.
- Serves 6.

WINE FOR LITTLE CHEESE PUFFS: *Sparkling wine is great with assorted finger foods; Sauvignon Blanc and Riesling would also be good with these.*

Elise's Potluck Potatoes

This dish is perfect to take to a pot-luck because you can make it up a day ahead, then cook it just before leaving the house. On the other hand, it can be reduced in size to make a full meal for a single person. It's delicious with ham. Leftovers reheat well.

6 large russet potatoes
1 bunch green onions
3 1/2 c. (625 ml) cheddar cheese
1 pt. (500 ml) sour cream
1 1/2 tsp. (8 ml) salt
1/2 tsp. (2 ml) black pepper

- Pre-heat oven to 350 F.
- Peel russet potatoes and cook for half the usual time. Shred or grate them into a large bowl.
- Slice green onions and grate the aged cheddar cheese.
- Combine everything except a half-cup of the cheese, which should be sprinkled over the top.
- Bake, uncovered, for 45 minutes.
- This could be made with low-fat sour cream and cheddar.
- Serves 15-20.

Thelma's Pecan Pie

This is as rich and delicious and sweet as a pie can be, especially if you love nuts as much as I do.

1 c. (250 ml) corn syrup
1 c. (250 ml) dark brown sugar
1/3 c. (75 ml) butter
1 c. (250 ml) pecans
3 eggs
1/2 tsp. (2 ml) vanilla
a pinch of salt
one nine-inch pie crust

- Pre-heat oven to 350 F.
- Combine corn syrup, dark brown sugar, melted butter, pecans, beaten eggs, vanilla and salt.
- Pour into an unbaked nine-inch pie shell and bake at 350F for 45 to 50 minutes.
- This could be topped with ice cream or whipped cream.

Mom's Sour Cream Pie

**If you're looking for a simple, but
tasty pie to make, look no further.**

1 c. (250 ml) sour cream
1 c. (250 ml) raisins
1 c. (250 ml) sugar
1 egg
1 tsp. (5 ml) vanilla
1/2 tsp. (2 ml) cinnamon
1/2 tsp. (2 ml) clove
a nine-inch pie shell

■ Preheat oven to 325 F.
■ Combine ingredients and pour into
   an unbaked pie shell.
■ Bake for about 30 minutes.
■ Serve while still warm.

14. Celebrate in Style

NEW YEAR'S NOSTALGIA

My recipe collection is bursting with flour-splattered and grease-splotched papers covered with the chicken scratches I've made over the years, along with the much-loved flowing strokes of my Mom's handwriting, (she was a school teacher), my dear aunt's very English scrawls, my godmother's flourish, friends' and acquaintances' familiar hands.

Some were penned by people I'll probably never see again, but they once meant enough that we shared a recipe or two, and memories take flight from that page.

In other cases these hand-written words are the closest I'll ever come again to people who occupied important niches in my life.

Passing recipes you love on to family or friends is an important tradition.

It's one that permits us to be immortalized, in a way, in the everyday lives of people we care about – even if their role in our lives was only to pass through it.

It's not only the recipes, it's the traditions and the occasions that they remind me of that make me nostalgic when I prepare certain dishes.

For French Canadians it could be the tortiere that adorns the table every Christmas Eve, or for the English, it could be the flaming rum pudding that was carried into the dining room to cap off the Christmas feast. (I can smell it now!)

As the year draws to a close and the shortest hours of light are marked by the Winter Solstice, we tend to entertain.

Some say it's the silliest time of year to do so, when roads are bad and weather unpredictable, but it's the time of year when we draw closer to other humans so that companionship and laughter can brighten the long winter evenings.

Food is always a focus of such special occasions, so plan ahead to prepare simple, but simply delicious foods to share with friends and family.

Don't forget that spicy salsa you bottled last summer. It will be excellent for a quick dip or a plate of natchos when a group of friends drops by; or a hostess gift if you're the guest.

Keep a few simple snacks prepared in the fridge or freezer, so you can re-heat or cook them up when company arrives. There are lots of good ideas in Chapter 13, Entertaining Eats.

Chicken Florentine with Brandied Mushrooms

The breading keeps the seasoned chicken breasts wonderfully moist and tender, and the mushrooms and brandy with browned butter is delectable over top. A special meal that's complemented nicely by a brown and wild rice side dish.

2 chicken breast halves
flour, salt and pepper to coat chicken
1 beaten egg
2 tbsp. (30 ml) parmesan
1/2 c. (125 ml) dry bread crumbs
1 bunch fresh spinach
1/4 lb. (100 g) mushrooms
1 tbsp. (15 ml) butter
1 tsp. (5 ml) olive oil
1/2 lemon
1 tbsp. (15 ml) butter
1 tbsp. (15 ml) brandy

- Prepare boned and skinned chicken breasts by first dredging in flour mixture, then beaten egg, then a mixture of dry bread crumbs and dried, grated parmesan cheese. Lay on a plate and refrigerate for an hour or so to firm up the coating.
- I use wax paper for both the flour and the crumb mixtures, and a shallow dish for the beaten egg. The paper can then just be thrown away.
- Thoroughly wash the spinach leaves, drain or spin dry and chop coarsely.
- Wash and slice mushrooms.
- Melt butter in a non-stick pan over medium heat and cook breaded chicken breasts, turning over when the underside is well-browned. Remove from the pan when they are just done and no pink remains in the thickest part.
- While they're cooking, lightly oil a wok or frypan. Put it on high heat and toss in the chopped spinach. Cook for about 30 seconds, or until just wilted.
- Remove spinach to a serving platter, squeeze fresh lemon juice over it, and keep warm.
- Arrange chicken on top when cooked, and keep warm.
- Melt remaining butter (not margarine or oil) in the pan the chicken was cooked in and quickly brown thinly-sliced mushrooms over high heat. Deglaze the pan with a spoonful or two of brandy, swirling it about in the pan with the browned butter and mushrooms. Drizzle it all over the chicken breasts and spinach.
- Serves 2.

See photograph on page **187**

WINE FOR CHICKEN FLORENTINE WITH BRANDIED MUSHROOMS: *This tasty dish calls for a Tempranillo, if you can find one (La Frenz, Inniskillin Okanagan or Stag's Hollow) or a red Meritage.*

Poached Snapper with Sherry

Using skim milk to make a sauce, flavoured with the fish and a touch of sherry is a good, low fat way to make a special meal.

1 1/2 lb. (700 g) red snapper
1 1/2 c. (375 ml) skim milk
3 whole cloves
6 peppercorns
sprig of dill
1/2 tsp. (2 ml) salt
3 green onions
2 tbsp. (30 ml) butter
2 tbsp. (30 ml) flour
freshly ground black pepper
2 tbsp. (30 ml) sherry
chopped chives, to garnish

- Poach pieces of snapper fillet in the mixture of milk, cloves, peppercorns, salt and a sprig of fresh herb such as dill, thyme or rosemary.
- Simmer for just a few minutes, until the thickest piece of the fish flakes easily. Lift fish out of the poaching liquid and put on a serving dish in a warm place while making the sauce.
- Mince green onions while the fish is cooking.
- I make the sauce in the microwave, but it can be done on the stovetop. Melt butter and cook chopped green onion for a few minutes. Stir in flour and cook, then slowly add the poaching liquid, whisking constantly, to make a thick white sauce.
- Season with salt and pepper, then add the sherry, stirring in well.
- Pour over fish in serving dish and garnish with a few chives.
- Serves 4.

See photograph on page **187**

WINE FOR POACHED SNAPPER WITH SHERRY:
I would serve a Chardonnay with a touch of the barrel to enhance its richness. For a special treat, find a Burrowing Owl Chardonnay or CedarCreek Platinum or Painted Rock Chardonnay or Jackson-Triggs SunRock Vineyard Chardonnay or Mission Hill SLC Chardonnay.

Beef & Spinach Casserole

This is a great dish for a potluck supper, or a meal in one dish for the family or for company. All the mess and dishes can be cleaned up ahead of time, then the casserole popped into the oven before guests arrive, or at the last minute, while you relax.

1 lb. lean ground beef
1 bag of spinach
1 c. (250 ml) mushrooms
1/2 c. (125 ml) Swiss cheese
1 egg
1/4 tsp. (1 ml) nutmeg
1/2 tsp. (2 ml) oregano
salt and pepper to taste
1 large onion
1/4 c. (60 ml) butter
1/4 c. (60 ml) flour
1 c. (250 ml) chicken stock
1 c. (250 ml) milk
2 c. (500 ml) pasta
1/4 c. (60 ml) Swiss cheese

■ Brown ground beef and wilt chopped spinach (the quantity isn't critical, so it's up to you) and sliced mushrooms. (I use a wok). Turn off the heat and add cheese, egg and spices.

■ Chop up onion and in another frypan, saute it in some of the butter until limp, then add the rest of the butter. When it's melted, add the flour, stir and cook for a minute.

■ Slowly add warmed chicken stock and whisk in well until it thickens, then gradually add milk to create a sauce.

■ Meanwhile cook pasta such as macaroni, shells, bow ties or cork-screws until just 'al dente.'

■ In a large greased casserole dish, layer pasta, ground beef mixture, sauce and then repeat, ending with sauce. Sprinkle the top with grated cheese.

■ Cook in a 350 F. oven for about 30 minutes.

■ Serves 4-6.

WINE FOR BEEF & SPINACH CASSEROLE: *Another time when the wine should not upstage the casserole but should be a good, uncomplicated red blend such as Cuvee Rouge from Domaine de Chaberton or Cuvee Noir from Gehringer Brothers.*

Chicken Rice with Chorizo & Prawns

This is full of different flavours, and despite the long list of ingredients, very quick to put together. Besides being nutritious, it's a complete meal in one pot. It's a very flexible recipe too. You can subtract all the meat and make it as a vegetarian dish, or add more or less of whichever are favourite ingredients in your house. It's a bit like paella.

WINE FOR CHICKEN RICE WITH CHORIZO & PRAWNS: *This calls for a bold red, like Orofino's Red Bridge Red or Inniskillin Okanagan's Dark Horse Vineyard Meritage or Stoneboat's Pinotage.*

4 chicken thighs
2 chorizo sausages
12 or so prawns
1 onion
8 mushrooms
2 celery ribs
1 red pepper
1 green pepper
4 tomatoes
2 garlic cloves
1 tbsp. (15 ml) olive oil
1 c. (250 ml) white rice
1 c. (250 ml) chicken stock
2 tbsp. (30 ml) fresh parsley
1 tsp. (5 ml) fresh thyme
1 tsp. (5 ml) salt
1/2 tsp. (2 ml) pepper
4 c. (500 ml) fresh spinach

- Bone and skin thighs and cut into bite-sized chunks. Slice up chorizo sausage and clean prawns.
- Chop onion, mushrooms, celery, peppers and tomatoes and mince garlic.
- Lightly brown the chicken and chorizo in olive oil over medium heat in a Dutch oven or deep frypan with a tight-fitting lid, cooking for just a few minutes. Push meat to one side and add onions to the pan.
- Cook and stir until softened, then add mushrooms and celery. Cook for a minute or two, then add the sweet peppers and garlic and cook, stirring, for another minute or two.
- Add the tomatoes, stirring and cooking for a minute before adding the rice, hot chicken stock, herbs, salt and pepper.
- Combine and return to bubbling, then push cleaned prawns into the top before covering tightly and putting into a 350 F oven, or turning the stovetop to its lowest setting.
- Cook for 15 minutes, stir in chopped fresh spinach and let sit for five minutes before serving.
- Serves 4 or 5.

Chicken Curry with Tomatoes

This is spicy, but not hot-spicy. That can be varied by adding chili peppers or hot red peppers to taste. As is, it has a wonderfully mellow flavor and should be served over rice so the sauce is put to good use.

2-3 lb. (1 kg) chicken thighs
2 tbsp. (30 ml) oil
2 c. (500 ml) onions
3 cloves garlic
1 tbsp. (15 ml) ginger root
1 tsp. (5 ml) cumin
1 tsp. (5 ml) coriander
1/2 tsp. (2 ml) chili powder
1/2 tsp. (2 ml) tumeric
1/2 c. (125 ml) water
1 c. (250 ml) chopped tomatoes
2 tbsp. (30 ml) fresh cilantro
1/2 c. (125 ml) plain yogurt
2 tsp. (10 ml) salt
1 tbsp. (15 ml) garam masala

■ Brown skinned chicken thighs in oil in a heavy Dutch oven over medium heat, then use a slotted spoon to remove them to a plate.

■ Dice onions, mince garlic and fresh ginger. Saute the onions, garlic and ginger in the remaining oil and stir constantly until the onions are limp. Reduce heat and add the spices and a splash of the water, stirring constantly until it's all well-mixed and cooking.

■ Stir in the chopped fresh or canned tomatoes, along with a tablespoon of the fresh cilantro, the yogurt and salt.

■ Return the chicken and its juices to the pot, add the remaining water and increase the heat until the whole mixture begins to bubble, turning the chicken pieces over until they're all covered with sauce. Add the garam masala, reduce the heat, cover the pot and simmer for half an hour or so until the chicken is tender.

■ Garnish with the remaining cilantro.

■ Serves 4-6.

Cauliflower Curry

This is a classic East Indian vegetable dish called Aloo Gobi, and doesn't need to accompany a curry dinner, but can be served with a grilled steak or other meat just as effectively.

1 small cauliflower
1 onion
2 medium potatoes
2 tbsp. (30 ml) oil
1 tsp. (5 ml) cumin
1 tsp. (5 ml) coriander
2 tsp. (10 ml) tumeric
1/2 tsp. (2 ml) salt
1/2 tsp. (2 ml) chili powder
1 tomato
1 tbsp. (15 ml) fresh ginger
1/4 c. (60 ml) water

- I'm a messy cook, so I use a wok with a lid to cook this in, but a frypan would work just fine, especially if you have someone to clean up after you.
- Separate the florets of the cauliflower and wash them. Chop the onion and the potatoes into half-inch chunks.
- Heat the oil and add the ground cumin, then the onion. Cook over medium to high heat for just a few minutes until soft. Add the potatoes and stir for a few minutes.
- Add the cauliflower and remaining spices and continue stirring.
- Add chopped-up tomato, finely chopped ginger and water. Cover and cook for 5 to 15 minutes, or until the vegetables are tender but not soggy.
- Serves 4.

Lamb Curry with Peas

This is a scrumptious way to serve lamb with lots of spicy flavour. It stays succulent and tender.

2 lb (1kg) lamb
2 tsp. (10 ml) coriander
1 tsp. (5 ml) cumin
1 tsp. (5 ml) salt
1 tsp. (5 ml) pepper
1/4 tsp. (1 ml) cayenne pepper
1 tbsp. (15 ml) cooking oil
1 tsp. (5 ml) brown mustard seeds
1 onion
1 tbsp. (15 ml) fresh ginger
1 tsp. (5 ml) garam masala
1 c. (250 ml) water
1 c. (250 ml) frozen peas
chopped fresh cilantro, to garnish

- Coat chopped, lean, boneless lamb meat in mixture of coriander, cumin, salt and peppers and let sit for a half-hour or so.
- Heat oil on medium heat in a wok or deep frypan, add mustard seeds and cover to keep them in the pan.
- Add thinly-sliced onion, minced fresh ginger and garam masala to the hot oil and stir until the onion is limp.
- Push to the sides and add the lamb. Cook and stir for a few minutes until the lamb is nice and brown.
- Stir in water and bring to bubbling. Cover and reduce the heat and let it simmer for nearly an hour, or until the lamb is nice and tender.
- Add frozen peas and heat through, letting the sauce boil up a bit if it seems too runny.
- Garnish with fresh cilantro before serving over fragrant basmati rice.
- Serves 4.

WINE FOR LAMB CURRY WITH PEAS: *I love curry dishes. There was a time when I liked them hot enough to make the glasses slide down the bridge of my nose. With curries like that, you want a crisp lager. With milder curries, a crisp Pinot Blanc is suitable, at least until someone releases British Columbia's first Grüner Veltliner.*

Winnie's Perogies

These are as light and delectable a perogy as I've ever tasted.

PEROGY DOUGH:
2/3 c. (150 ml) warm water
1/2 c. (125 ml) warm milk
1 tbsp. (15 ml) butter
1 egg
3 c. (750 ml) flour
1 tsp. (5 ml) salt

POTATO FILLING:
1 small onion
2 tbsp. (30 ml) butter
5 c. (1.25 l) mashed potatoes
2 c. (500 ml) shredded cheddar cheese
salt and pepper, to taste

WINE FOR WINNIE'S PEROGIES:
Once again, I like Pinot Blanc with perogies.

- To make the dough, combine water, milk, butter and egg and beat well. Slowly stir in flour and salt. Knead dough on a floured board for a couple of minutes, until smooth and soft.
- Place in lightly-oiled bowl; cover and let rest for 30 minutes.
- Meanwhile, prepare the filling by frying the finely chopped onion in butter. Add to the mashed potatoes when they're nice and soft and stir in the cheese and season to taste. You may substitute dry curd cottage cheese for the cheddar.
- Working with a third of the dough at a time, roll out on a floured surface, about 1/8th inch thick.
- Cut three-inch circles of dough, about three inches in diameter.
- Place a rounded teaspoon of filling in the centre of each circle, held in one hand.
- Fold the dough up around the filling, forming a half circle and pinching the edges together with your fingers to seal in the filling.
- Place on a clean tea towel and cover to prevent them from drying out.
- Bring a large pot of salted water to a boil and put 10 or 12 perogies at a time into the water, stirring a bit to prevent sticking.
- Simmer three to five minutes after they float to the top.
- Remove with a slotted spoon to a platter, in a single layer, or add butter and toss to prevent them from sticking to each other.
- Serve with sour cream or plain yogurt, bacon bits or chopped, fried onions, or green onions.
- I like them pan-fried slowly in a little butter, until golden.

See photograph on page **188**

Apple & Cranberry-stuffed Pork

There are layers of flavour in this stuffing and all of them go well with pork. It also helps to keep lean pork tender and not dry.

2 lb. (1 kg) boneless pork roast
1 apple
1 small onion
2 tsp. (10 ml) fresh ginger
1 tbsp. (15 ml) fresh sage
2 tsp. (10 ml) tarragon
1/8 tsp. (.5 ml) cayenne
1 c. (250 ml) bread cubes
1 tbsp. (15 ml) sherry
1/4 c. (60 ml) cranberries
salt and pepper, to taste

- Have your butcher double-butterfly a nice lean pork loin roast, or do it yourself with a couple of careful cuts.
- If it's uneven in thickness, pound it gently to even it out and sprinkle with a little salt.
- Core apple; then finely chop apple and onion and mince fresh ginger and herbs.
- Cook onion and ginger in a drizzle of olive oil in a deep pan or wok until it's just soft and add chopped apple, turning about for a minute, then removing from heat.
- Add small, dried bread cubes and sprinkle with sherry or apple juice.
- Add herbs, cayenne and salt and pepper, to taste; then mix well.
- Spread evenly over the pork and dot with whole, unsweetened cranberries, fresh or frozen.
- Roll up the meat and carefully place in a roasting pan which has been lightly sprayed with oil.
- Roast for about 45 minutes, checking for doneness and removing as soon as the pork is cooked.
- Slice into pinwheels and drizzle any juices from the pan over the meat on the serving dish or board.
- Serve immediately.
- Serves 4 or 5.

See photograph on page **188**

WINE FOR APPLE & CRANBERRY-STUFFED PORK: *I really like a good Pinot Noir with lean pork loin. There are so many good producers in British Columbia including Foxtrot, Meyer Family Vineyards, Howling Bluff, Quails' Gate, CedarCreek, Seven Stones, Averill Creek and Mt. Lehman.*

Bernice's Chocolate Orange Marble

This classy-looking, delectable, rich dessert of chocolate and orange can be made ahead of time and frozen, ready for that special occasion.

1/4 c. (60 ml) butter
1 c. (250 ml) chocolate wafer
  crumbs
2 eggs
1/2 c. (125 ml) sugar
8 oz. (225 g) cream cheese
1 c. (250 ml) heavy cream
1/2 tsp. (2 ml) orange zest
2/3 c. (150 ml) chocolate chips

- Melt butter and mix well with chocolate wafer crumbs.
- Press mixture into the bottom of a nine-inch square pan.
- Separate eggs. Beat sugar, egg yolks and cream cheese until smooth.
- Beat egg whites until soft peaks form. Whip cream. Carefully fold egg whites and whipped cream into cheese mixture.
- Divide in half. Grate orange zest, and fold into one half of mixture. Melt chocolate chips and fold into the other half of mixture.
- Layer onto crumb crust and zigzag a knife through the mixture, without disturbing the crust, to create a marbled effect.
- Freeze until ready to serve.

15. Cheap and Easy

QUICK CLASSICS

It's amazing what a cook with a little time and imagination can do with a bunch of bones.

Soups and stews are like a canvas to a painter: once you have the background basics in place, your own taste and creativity can take over to paint a palette of flavours.

As long as you have a container of stock in the freezer, you have the canvas for new works of art for the family table.

Soup can be a progressive thing, too. If you begin with the stock, then add fresh vegetables for lunch the first day, and you've got Meal One.

For Meal Two, make meatballs and add them to the re-warmed soup. Toss a fresh salad on the side and you have dinner.

Add a jar of your summer tomatoes and some zucchini, cauliflower or eggplant for a meal on the third day, and you've got more than your money's worth from a simple bunch of bones.

Somehow there's nothing quite like a welcoming bowl of hot soup after a day working out in the cold, skiing or just shovelling the walk.

Soup made one day always seems better on the next, so make enough for at least two meals. It will be great for days when everyone's too busy to make dinner from scratch.

It feels just like going out, but it's much less expensive and probably more nutritious, too.

Winter weather makes your insides long for comfort food like hot soups and stews. What better time to toss together the ingredients for a home made soup stock when it's snowing so hard outside you need a rope to find your way back from the barn after you've milked the cow?

Even skiers, snowboarders and snowmobilers have to spend some in-time on their off-days when there's a blizzard raging. Before you delve into your favorite book, or put your feet up in front of a blazing fire, combine the ingredients for a later lunch or dinner, and let it simmer on the stove while you relax.

With today's busy lives, time is sometimes the rarest ingredient in an old-fashioned, home made meal.

Once made, stock can be frozen in ziplock bags or recycled margarine tubs, ready for use as needed. If you know you'll want a particular amount for a future soup, freeze it in that quantity, all ready to use.

Beef Stock

We use stocks in all sorts of cooking, from rice pilaf to soups and stews; from sauces to gravies. You'd be surprised at the difference in the flavour between home made ones and commercial stocks.

2 lb. (1 kg) soup bones
2 onions
1 stalk celery
1 carrot
1 bay leaf
4 peppercorns
2 garlic cloves
1 tsp. (5 ml) salt
water

- Preheat oven to 425 F.
- Put bones into a pan. Place them in the preheated oven and roast for 40 minutes, turning once. Remove from oven and place the bones in a large Dutch oven along with the chopped onion, celery, carrot and seasonings. Cover it all with water and bring to a boil. Reduce the heat and simmer with a cover on for another 2 hours.
- Strain stock into a large bowl, discarding the bones, bay leaf and vegetables. Refrigerate the strained stock until it's cold, then lift and discard any fat that has risen to the surface. Use within 3 days or freeze up to three months.

Chicken Stock

The next time you de-bone chicken breasts, save the bones with the remaining meat clinging to them; purchase necks and backs from your butcher; remove the backs from your next package of chicken parts, or buy a cheap stewing bird to toss into the stock pot.

1 boiling fowl
1 stalk celery
1 onion
1 carrot
2 bay leaves
1 tsp. (5 ml) parsley
1 tsp. (5 ml) salt
dash of pepper
water

- Cut chicken into pieces and place all the pieces into a large pot. Add enough water to cover the chicken. Cover the pot and bring to a boil, lower heat and skim off any froth that boils up.
- Coarsely chop celery, onion and carrot. Add remaining ingredients and simmer until the chicken is done.
- Remove the chicken and set aside to use the meat in a chicken pie or dice for chicken sandwiches. Discard the bay leaves and strain the stock into a large bowl. Use the stock immediately or freeze it for future use.

Den's Meatloaf

This is moist and flavorful, quick and simple to make after work, and the whole family will love it. You may substitute any ground game meat for the ground beef.

1 lb. (454 g) lean ground beef
1 large onion
1 stalk celery
drizzle of oil
1 egg
1 clove garlic
1/4 c. (60 ml) chili sauce
2 tbsp. (30 ml) ketchup
1 tbsp. (15 ml) worcestershire
1/4 c. (60 ml) oat bran or
bread crumbs
10 drops hot sauce
1/2 tsp. (2 ml) pepper
1/2 tsp. (2 ml) salt

TOPPING:
1 large potato
1/2 c. (125 ml) cheddar cheese

- Pre-heat oven to 350 F.
- Chop onion and celery and saute it in a pan with a drizzle of oil, over medium heat, until softened.
- Mince garlic.
- Beat egg in a medium-sized bowl and combine all remaining ingredients, including the onion mixture. At this point add spinach and chopped mushrooms or diced sweet peppers, if you like (See variations, below.)
- Pack into a loaf pan and bake for about 45 minutes.
- Meanwhile, microwave a whole potato for about five minutes, or cook it in the oven beside the meatloaf, then remove. Cool and slice it.
- Layer it on top of the meat, then sprinkle cheddar cheese over it, and cook a further 15 minutes.
- Serves 4.

See photograph on page **205**

Meatloaf Variations

Everyone makes a different sort of meatloaf it seems, but there are a few basic variations which can make quite a difference in flavor or presentation:

For instance, when you pack your meatloaf mixture into a loaf pan, put half in first, then place a row of hard-cooked eggs down the centre before packing the remainder on top, for a really dramatic sliced meatloaf.

Mashed potatoes may be substituted for the potato slices, with or without the cheese.

For a different flavor, make up a quick bread stuffing. Add herbs such as sage and thyme to the onions and the bread crumbs, and layer it in the loaf pan alternately with the remainder of the meat mixture. In this case, omit the cheese, and sprinkle a few bread crumbs over the top instead.

Mushrooms make a nice addition to a meatloaf recipe, and can also be arranged attractively on top either with or without cheddar cheese.

Spinach is delicious in a meatloaf. Just shred fresh spinach and mix in with the meat mixture; or use a package of thawed frozen spinach to mix in with the other ingredients.

Finely-chopped green and red peppers are nice added to the mixture as well.

See photograph on page **205**

WINE FOR MEAT LOAF:
Meat loaf is a flavour chameleon that supports just about any red you have on hand. For a change of pace, open a Malbec from Inniskillin or La Frenz or Quinta Ferreira.

WINE FOR MOM'S PEA SOUP:
This calls for a mug of ale.

Mom's Pea Soup

Mom was famous for her delicious pea soup. It's a complete meal in a bowl with a whole wheat roll on the side.

1 ham bone
2 c. (500 ml) yellow split peas
2 c. (500 ml) onions
1 c. (250 ml carrots
1 c. (250 ml) celery
1 tsp. (5 ml) thyme
1/4 tsp. (1 ml) cayenne

- Soak the dried split peas for about half an hour in enough water to cover them well.
- Place ham bone, complete with any meat remaining on it, in a large soup pot. (You may substitute a couple of pork hocks, and add a chicken or turkey carcass.)
- Add chopped onions, carrots and celery, the peas with the water they were soaked in, and the seasonings.
- Add water to bring the amount of liquid up to two or three quarts.
- Bring to a boil, then reduce to simmering and cover for three or four hours.
- Remove bones, then press the stock through a sieve or blend the vegetables and stock until smooth.
- Cool and remove the fat that rises to the top.
- Taste for seasoning and add salt and pepper if needed.
- Re-heat to serve.

Cheese, Onion & Beer Bread

This looks rustic and old-fashioned, and is wonderful served right from the oven for a special meal. It's perfect with soups.

2 3/4 c. (675 ml) flour
1 tbsp. (15 ml) baking powder
1 tbsp. (15 ml) sugar
1/2 tsp. (2 ml) salt
1/2 tsp. (2 ml) cracked black pepper
1 c. (250 ml) grated cheddar
2 green onions
1 small onion
1/4 c. (60 ml) grated cheddar
1 tbsp (15 ml) sesame seeds
1 can or bottle of beer

- Grease a 9x5-inch loaf pan.
- Pre-heat oven to 350 F.
- Combine dry ingredients in a large bowl, then stir in grated well-aged cheddar cheese and finely-chopped green onions.
- Thinly slice a small onion, and have the other quarter-cup of grated cheddar and the sesame seeds handy.
- Add room temperature beer to the dry ingredients and stir just until mixed in.
- Scrape the dough out into the loaf pan, arrange onion slices on top, then grated cheese, and sprinkle with sesame seeds.
- Bake for 50-60 minutes, then let stand on a wire rack for five minutes before removing from pan.
- Let cool a few minutes more before slicing and serving.

Spicy Tomato Veggie Pasta

The beauty of this is it can all be served in one dish, it's very quick to make and it's also very versatile: you can omit the sausage for a vegetarian version, and add a bit more cheese; or vary the herbs to your taste; or use a milder sausage, or a different cheese. All of the quantities can be changed: add more pasta or sausage if you'd prefer, or more spinach.

1 c. uncooked pasta:
    corkscrew, penne or other
1 onion
drizzle of oil
2 chorizo sausages
4 c. baby spinach leaves
14 oz. (398 ml) diced tomatoes
1 tsp. (5 ml) fresh oregano
1 tsp. (5 ml) fresh basil
handful of grated mozzarella cheese
garnish with grated parmesan cheese

- Cook pasta al dente and drain.
- Chop onion and cook until softened, in a drizzle of oil in a deep frypan. Add thinly-sliced chorizo sausage pieces and cook through.
- Add spinach and stir until limp. Add a tin of tomatoes, or chopped, fresh ones with minced fresh herbs and heat through.
- Sprinkle grated mozzarella cheese over the hot pasta, either in individual bowls, or a large serving bowl, and spoon the meat and tomato mixture over top, then garnish with parmesan cheese.
- Serves 4.

See photograph on page **205**

WINE FOR SPICY TOMATO VEGGIE PASTA:
Serve a medium-bodied red like Prospect's Merlot Cabernet.

TOP:
Fruit Crisp
Recipe on
page 154

BOTTOM:
**Pat's
Gingerbread**
Recipe on
page 160

TOP:
Pork & Shrimp Pot Stickers
Recipe on page **163**

BOTTOM:
Cheddar Pennies
Recipe on page **165**

TOP:
**Chicken
Florentine**

Recipe on
page **170**

BOTTOM:
**Poached
Snapper**

Recipe on
page **171**

TOP:
Winnie's Perogies
Recipe on
page **177**

BOTTOM:
Apple & Cranberry-stuffed Pork
Recipe on
page **178**

Super Sunny Muffins

These muffins are packed with fruit, vegetables, seeds, nuts, grains and protein, yet despite how good they are for you, everyone always raves about how good they taste.

Make lots because people always come back for more. The recipe doubles well.

There are so many ways this recipe can be varied it's hard to keep up. They're great as a breakfast on the run, a snack or light lunch to take along wherever you go.

Try using the locally-grown, little blue Coronation grapes available at fruit stands and in stores. I freeze them in the fall for adding to muffins and loaves all winter. Delicious.

1 c. (250 ml) whole wheat flour
1/2 c.(125 ml) brown sugar
1 tsp. (5 ml) baking soda
1 tsp. (5 ml) cinnamon
1/2 c. (125 ml) grated carrot
1/2 c. (125 ml) grapes or apple
1/2 mashed banana
1/6 c. (40 ml) sunflower seeds
1/6 c. (40 ml) chocolate chips
2 eggs
1/2 c. oil

- Pre-heat oven to 375 F. Grease 12 muffin cups.
- Mix the dry ingredients together well in a large bowl, and add carrots, chopped or grated apples, other fruit, seeds and chips.
- Beat eggs in a smaller bowl and add oil.
- Stir wet and dry ingredients together until just moistened and spoon into muffin cups.
- Bake for 15-20 minutes.

ALTERNATIVES:
- *Instead of all whole wheat flour, you could substitute 1/4 cup of cornmeal, oat bran or wheat germ for 1/4 cup of the flour.
- *Grated apples could be used instead of carrots, or substituted for half the carrots.
- *Add up to two tablespoons of chopped-up dried apricots or coconut to recipe.
- *Use half the oil, substituting water and skim milk powder for the other half.

See photograph on page **206**

Ginger & Chickpea Salad

Fresh, minced ginger gives the crisp chickpeas a delicious, refreshing lift and the chili powder adds a nice spiciness. This makes a great lunch or light supper, and because the dressing is part of the salad's marinade, it's a great lunch to take to work or school. Chick peas or garbanzo beans are a good source of vegetable protein and fibre.

1 can chick peas
2 stalks celery
4 green onions
1 tbsp. (15 ml) fresh ginger
1 tbsp. (15 ml) fresh parsley
1 clove garlic
1/2 tsp. (2 ml) chili powder
1/4 tsp. (1 ml) cayenne pepper
2 tbsp. (30 ml) olive oil
2 tbsp. (30 ml) wine vinegar
salt and pepper to taste
lettuce leaves

- Rinse chick peas well and drain. If using dried ones, re-constitute first. The quantity isn't critical.
- Slice celery lengthwise a couple of times, then chop into dice. Chop green onions and mince ginger and parsley. Smush garlic and mince.
- Combine all ingredients except lettuce and let sit in the refrigerator overnight or for a few hours so the flavours can marry.
- Serve over crisp, fresh, green lettuce leaves.
- Serves 2-4.

Mom's Butterscotchies

These are sweet like candy and delicious, but ever so quick to make. There's no flour in them, and I make them and mix them in the same pan. No dirty bowls.

1 c. (250 ml) butter
1 c. (250 ml) brown sugar
1/2 tsp. (2 ml) soda
2 c. (500 ml) rolled oats
1 tsp. (5 ml) vanilla

- Combine butter and sugar in a large pan, 8x10x2, and heat, but do not allow to boil.
- Add soda and stir until mixture has the consistency of honey.
- Remove from heat and add rolled oats and vanilla.
- Bake in a slow oven, 300 F, for 20-25 minutes.
- Carefully cut into squares before it cools off.

Soy Chicken

This melts off the bones when made in the crock pot, but my kids always thought it was heavenly. It seems like a lot of soy sauce for one dish, but the sauce it's cooked in can be frozen and re-used many times, as long as you handle it carefully and never leave it at room temperature.

WINE FOR SOY CHICKEN:
The saltiness of soy sauce does not sit well with most wines. I think apple cider or ale would be preferable.

1 chicken
2 c. (500 ml) soy sauce
1/4 c. (60 ml) dry sherry
knob fresh ginger
2 cloves garlic
2 tbsp. (30 ml) brown sugar
water, as needed

- Use a pot or slow cooker in which a chicken will fit snugly.
- Clean and trim any fat from an economical bird. Combine soy, sherry and brown sugar in the pot; heat and stir to dissolve the sugar.
- Peel and chop a one-inch knob of fresh ginger, and crush and peel the garlic. Add both to the sauce.
- Place the chicken in the pot and add enough water to bring the liquid at least half-way up the side of the bird, probably a cup or two.
- Bring to boiling, then turn the bird over in the sauce, using tongs or a large fork and spoon.
- If it's a crock pot, cover and cook on low for five or six hours.
- If in a Dutch oven or similar pot, put in the oven at 325 F for a couple of hours, turning it again in its sauce half-way through that time.
- Serve whole on a platter, or carefully cut into pieces for serving, pouring a few spoonfuls of the sauce over it before cooling and freezing the cooking liquid for next time.
- A dish of stir-fried vegetables rounds out the meal for four, or this could become part of a Chinese meal for many more people.

Mideast Chicken

This is a great dish to serve when you have company because it can be made ahead, and leaves you free to entertain friends or family while it finishes up in the oven.

4 lb. (2 kg) chicken thighs
flour
salt and pepper
drizzle of oil
1 large onion
2 cloves garlic
1 tsp. (5 ml) fresh ginger
1 lemon
2 tomatoes
1 c. (250 ml) chicken stock
1/2 tsp. (2 ml) ground cumin
1/2 tsp. (2 ml) pepper
fresh parsley or cilantro, to garnish

- Pre-heat oven to 350F.
- Coat the chicken parts with flour seasoned with salt and pepper and brown in a drizzle of hot oil in the frypan or Dutch oven you plan to cook it in.
- Chop onion and mince garlic and fresh ginger. Cut lemon and tomatoes into wedges.
- Remove chicken, reduce heat and add chopped onions, garlic and ginger to the pan. Add a drizzle of oil if needed, and cook for a few minutes until softened and translucent.
- Add chicken stock and stir to remove any brown bits from the bottom of the pan as you bring it to bubbling. Add seasonings and half the lemon wedges.
- Return chicken pieces to sauce, or pour sauce over chicken in a casserole dish.
- Garnish with the tomato wedges and remaining lemon wedges, then cover and bake in a 350 F oven for about an hour. You may also turn it to the lowest heat, cover and cook on top of the stove.
- Remove lemon wedges and sprinkle with chopped fresh parsley or cilantro.
- Serves 4-6.

Bulgur Pilaf

This is great served with the Mideast Chicken, but it also re-heats beautifully. It's even better eaten cold with the addition of fresh vegetables such as tomatoes and pepper, plus a sprinkle of olive oil and lemon juice and minced fresh herbs.

WINE FOR BULGUR PILAF:
A Gamay Noir or a full-flavoured rosé would be my choice with this dish.

1 large onion
1/4 c. (60 ml) fresh parsley
1 tbsp. (15 ml) fresh thyme
1 carrot
1 celery stalk
olive oil, as needed
2 c. (500 ml) bulgur
salt and pepper to taste
3 c. (750 ml) chicken stock
fresh parsley, to garnish

- Chop onion and mince parsley and thyme. Thinly slice carrot and celery.
- Heat a generous drizzle of olive oil on medium heat in a deep lidded frypan or casserole dish.
- Add bulgur, cooking and stirring constantly over medium heat until lightly brown. Remove bulgur to a bowl and add another drizzle of olive oil to the pan.
- Cook onion, carrot and celery, turning and stirring until all are softened.
- Return bulgur to pan along with hot chicken stock, fresh herbs and salt and pepper to taste.
- Bring to bubbling, then reduce the heat to the lowest possible temperature, cover tightly and cook for 15 minutes or so, until all the liquid has been absorbed.
- Remove from heat and leave covered for 10 minutes before gently lifting to mix, then serve.
- Garnish with fresh parsley.

Spinach Cannelloni with Cheese

This is my favourite Italian dish. You could add a half-pound lean ground meat or a half-pound of seafood to the filling if you wish.

12 lasagne noodles

FILLING:
1 small onion
1 large garlic clove
1 tbsp. (15 ml) olive oil
10 oz. (284 g) spinach
1 large egg
1 tsp.(5 ml) fresh oregano
1 lb. (454 g) ricotta cheese
salt and pepper to taste

TOPPING:
2 c. (500 ml) tomato sauce
2 c. (500 ml) white sauce
1/2 lb. (250 g) mozzarella cheese

- Cook noodles according to package directions, Don't overcook. Cut each in half and lay out on a board or the counter, ready to roll up around the filling.
- Meanwhile, chop onion and mince garlic. Mince oregano and grate cheese.
- Heat olive oil in a frypan and cook onion and garlic until limp.
- If using fresh spinach, chop and add to the pan, turning about until it's just limp. If using frozen, thaw it first and squeeze it dry, chop and add to pan, cooking just until the moisture has evaporated.
- I generally use a large wok for this, then take it off the heat and add the remaining ingredients to mix, but you could just dump the spinach mixture into a large bowl and add the rest of the ingredients. Mix well.
- Divide filling into 24 portions and put a dab on the bottom third of each half piece of lasagne noodle.
- Spread about a half-cup of your favourite tomato sauce on the bottom of a 9x14 inch pan or oven-safe dish, or two smaller ones.
- Pre-heat oven to 375 F.
- Roll filling up in pasta and lay each, seam side down, in the prepared dish.
- Pour white sauce over the rolls, top it with the remaining tomato sauce, then grated mozzarella cheese.
- Bake, uncovered, for about half an hour, or until everything's bubbling and the top's slightly browned.
- Slide under the broiler for a few minutes if it isn't as brown as you like.
- Makes about 24 cannelloni.
- Freezes well.

WINE FOR SPINACH CANNELLONI WITH CHEESE:
I would like a Sangiovese or a Tempranillo with this. Look to Inniskillin Okanagan and Sandhill for these.

16. For Healthy Hearts

STIR-FRY INTO NEW YEAR

Food is often a memorable part of cultural occasions and personal celebrations, whether that's a birthday or the start of a new year.

And, food brings people together to share, so I'm always in favour of celebrating whatever occasion comes along, whether it's a part of my heritage or not—with food.

Deep in a B.C. winter, there are two noteworthy occasions, both brightly focussed on the colour red, and both marked by food traditions: Chinese New Year and Valentine's Day.

The Chinese (lunar) calendar is based on moon cycles rather than on days as the Western (solar) calendar is. The date varies between Jan. 20 and Feb. 20, but it's always on the second new moon after Dec. 22, the winter solstice.

For weeks ahead of the Chinese New Year, tradition demands that everyone cleans house—in more ways than one. Quarrels are to be patched up so all can welcome in the new year on a fresh footing.

Celebrations continue for about two weeks, until the moon is full, concluding with a Lantern Festival.

Little red packets of money are given to the children for good luck. In fact, the color red, because of its bright and happy tone, is predominant.

The preparation of large amounts of food symbolizes abundance and wealth for the household.

Asian cuisine tends to be lean, nutritious, delicious, economical, versatile and appealing.

Stir-fried dishes include a wide variety of crisp vegetables, with a little lean meat and just a drizzle of oil.

They're also very attractive, with a variety of colours from the different vegetables. They should never be overcooked, or they turn greyish, and lose their vibrancy.

Regulating cooking time helps vegetables retain their flavour and protects the vitamin content too. Some vitamins are degraded by excess heat.

Whether you serve such dishes over rice or noodles is up to you.

Because everything is cooked very quickly it's important to have all ingredients prepared in advance and nearby. Begin with the ingredients which will take the longest to cook and don't add the most delicate ones, like bean sprouts, until the very end. Remember that food continues cooking for a few minutes after it's removed from the heat.

A wok is the best utensil for such cooking, but a deep frypan can work.

Many Oriental sauces are now available in supermarkets or in specialty stores. Try a few different ones and see which you like best; mix and match.

We feast first with our eyes, so remember to garnish with nuts, seeds or minced green onions for an attractive finish. With Chinese stir-fry recipes, don't hesitate to substitute.

Enjoy, and Gung Hay Fat Choy!

Chicken with Ginger & Vegetables

Lean chicken and lots of vegetables equal plenty of flavour. Serve over long noodles, uncut so you'll have good luck in the new year. Sugar peas or asparagus, in season, are delicious in this. You could substitute hoisin or Chinese barbecue sauce for the Chee Hou Sauce. Use chicken breast instead of thighs if you wish.

2 boneless chicken thighs
2 tsp. (10 ml) soy sauce
2 tsp. (10 ml) cornstarch
1 tbsp. (15 ml) minced ginger

1 small onion
1 celery stalk
1 small zucchini
6 small mushrooms
handful of spinach leaves
1/4 red pepper
1 tbsp. (15 ml) minced ginger
drizzle of oil
1 tbsp. (15 ml) Chee Hou Sauce
1 tsp. (5 ml) Szechuan sauce
1/2 -1 c. (125-250 ml) water
2 tsp. (10 ml) cornstarch
2 tsp. (10 ml) cold water
garnish with a few cashew nuts

- Slice boneless chicken into thin strips and marinate in the mixture of soy, cornstarch and minced, fresh ginger for a few hours.
- Half onion, set it flat side down and slice into strips; slice celery and zucchini, mushrooms and spinach, dice red pepper and mince the second spoonful of ginger.
- Combine cornstarch and cold water in a tiny bowl and set aside.
- Heat a drizzle of oil in a wok over medium-high heat and add the minced ginger and onion and stir fry. Add sliced celery, zucchini and mushrooms and continue to stir fry.
- Remove to a bowl, a serving dish or the wok lid.
- Add another drizzle of oil to the wok and dump chicken mixture in, spreading it out and letting it brown for a minute. Stir fry until no longer pink and then add Oriental sauces. Begin to add water, stirring and bringing to a boil. Add re-combined cornstarch and cold water mixture and bring to a bubble, then add just enough water so a nice thick sauce is created once it begins to simmer again.
- Return vegetables to the wok and stir together just until they're coated with sauce.
- Add a few cashew nuts, if desired, and serve hot.
- Serves 2 or 3.

WINE FOR CHICKEN WITH GINGER & VEGETABLES: *I would like an exotic wine with this, notably Calona Vineyard's Sovereign Opal, fruity with aromas of rose petals and spice. Sovereign Opal is a varietal that was created in British Columbia and exclusive to Calona.*

Peanut Chicken

This is a yummy mixture of mellow peanuts, soy and sesame. You may substitute whatever vegetables sound good with this and are available. For instance a few snow peas or a bag of spinach would be excellent tossed in at the last minute because they are really good with a peanut sauce.

WINE FOR PEANUT CHICKEN:
The flavours would challenge grape wines, I think, so I recommend a fruit wine, perhaps Forbidden Fruit's Cherysh Cherry Rosé or Sleeping Giant's Cherry Wine.

3 boneless chicken thighs
1 tbsp. (15 ml) light soy sauce
1/4 tsp. (1 ml) sesame oil
2 tsp. (10 ml) dry sherry

6 spears asparagus
4 mushrooms
1 celery stalk
1 onion
drizzle of oil
1/2 c. (125 ml) water
1 tbsp. (15 ml) teriyaki sauce
2 tbsp. (30 ml) crunchy peanut butter
1 tbsp. (15 ml) cornstarch
1 tbsp. (15 ml) cold water
2 tbsp. (30 ml) toasted sesame seeds

- Slice boneless chicken thighs or breasts into thin strips and marinate for several minutes or a few hours in a mix of light soy sauce, sesame oil and dry sherry (you may substitute rice wine, apple juice or water).
- Meanwhile, chop asparagus into one-inch lengths, after removing the tough ends; slice mushrooms, celery and onion and set aside in piles on your work area. Combine cornstarch and cold water in a tiny bowl and set aside.
- Have remaining ingredients handy.
- Drizzle a little cooking oil in a wok set on medium-high heat and add the onion and stir-fry for a minute; add the celery and stir; then the mushrooms, and finally, the asparagus.
- Add the water and cover to steam for a minute or two, but don't overcook.
- Remove from wok to lid, a bowl, or the serving plate and add another drizzle of oil to the wok.
- Add the marinated chicken and stir fry for a few minutes until white and firm.
- Add teriyaki sauce and peanut butter to the middle of the wok and combine, then stir into the chicken, adding a little water if necessary.
- Push it up the side of the wok, bring the liquid in the bottom to bubbling and add the combination of cornstarch and water, stirring until it thickens and turns translucent.
- Add the vegetables back and stir everything together until it's all covered with a glaze of sauce.
- Garnish with sesame seeds.
- Serves 3-4.

Tofu & Ginger Vegetables

This is a very flavourful way to serve fresh vegetables without meat. Tofu is an excellent source of protein, and is delicious with a sauce. However, add a half pound of lean, ground pork or slivers of lean pork to this if you wish. Shredded cabbage is also delicious added with the onions.

3/4 lb. (350 g) block firm tofu
1 tbsp. (15 ml) fresh ginger
1 onion
1 red pepper
1 c. (250 ml) peas
1 tbsp. (15 ml) ground bean sauce
1/2 tsp. (3 ml) szechuan sauce
drizzle of oil
1/2-1 c. (125-250 ml) water
1 tbsp. (15 ml) cornstarch
1 tbsp. (15 ml) cold water

- Rinse and cut firm tofu (bean curd) into half to one-inch squares and set aside.
- Mince ginger and chop onion into medium-sized squares, and cut red pepper similarly.
- Fresh peas are delicious, but use frozen ones if they're not available.
- Combine cornstarch with an equal amount of water in a tiny bowl and set aside.
- Both ground (or brown) bean sauce and Szechuan sauce are available at local markets in the Oriental ingredients section.

- Heat a drizzle of oil on high heat in a large pan or wok suitable for stir-frying.
- Just before it begins to smoke, drop in the ginger and turn a couple of times to flavour the oil before adding tofu squares.
- Let them brown, but not burn, on all sides, turning carefully every few minutes, then remove to a serving dish.
- Immediately add onions, stir fry for a few minutes, then add red pepper and peas, stir frying for just a minute or so, until the onion is soft and the other vegetables become brighter in colour, but not soft in texture.
- Add sauces and combine with vegetables, then add water, stir-frying until it's mixed in.
- Move vegetables away from the centre of the wok, and when the liquid begins to bubble, add the re-combined cornstarch mixture, stirring until the sauce thickens and becomes translucent.
- Quickly combine with vegetables and pour over tofu cubes in serving dish.
- Serves 2-4.

See photograph on page **206**

WINE FOR TOFU & GINGER VEGETABLES:
How about Perrier or San Pelligrino sparkling mineral waters?

Bok Choy with Mushrooms & Ginger

Crisp and colourful, this vegetable dish tastes as good as it looks, but it's vital that none of the vegetables are overcooked.

1 large onion
1 knob ginger
6 baby bok choy
12 mushrooms
1 red pepper
2 c. (500 ml) bean sprouts
1 tbsp. (15 ml) soy sauce
1/2 c. (125 ml) chicken stock
1/2 tsp. (2 ml) sugar
oil
2 tbsp. (30 ml) cold water
1 tbsp. (15 ml) cornstarch
salt and pepper to taste
sesame seeds, to garnish

WINE FOR BOK CHOY WITH MUSHROOMS & GINGER:
I would pour a crisp lager or a dry but fruity white like the Chasselas/Pinot Blanc/Pinot Gris from Quails' Gate.

- Slice onion into about 8 wedges, separate layers and mince ginger.
- Rinse bok choy, mushrooms, pepper and bean sprouts.
- Depending on the size of the baby bok choy, remove largest stems and chop into large chunks, but leave the baby stems in the centre whole.
- Quarter mushrooms and chop pepper into large chunks.
- Dissolve cornstarch in cold water in a small bowl and set aside.
- Combine chicken stock, soy and sugar in a small bowl and set aside.

- Heat oil in a wok or deep frypan over medium-high heat, then add minced ginger, stir about and add onion.
- Stir and fry for a minute or so before adding mushrooms. Stir for another minute or so.
- Add bok choy, stir, then make sure base of each whole baby bok choy is facing down in the pan and the green part is closer to the rim.
- Sprinkle peppers and bean sprouts over the top of vegetables.
- Add chicken stock mixture and bring to a boil. Cover and steam for just a couple of minutes.
- Re-combine cornstarch mixture, move vegetables to sides of pan or wok and add it to the liquid in the middle, bringing it to bubbling and stirring until the sauce is thickened and smooth.
- Add salt and pepper , if needed, to taste, and combine everything briefly.
- Turn out onto a platter, sprinkle with sesame seeds, and serve.

Black Bean Beef

You can purchase the sauce already made up, or make your own, purchasing just the dried fermented black beans, ready to squish together with minced garlic, fresh ginger and soy sauce.

1/2 lb. (225 g) beef strips
1 tbsp. (15 ml) soy
1 tbsp. (15 ml) sherry
1 tbsp. (15 ml) cornstarch
1 large onion
12 asparagus stalks
1 small zucchini
8 mushrooms
diced sweet peppers, to taste
3 tbsp. (45 ml) dried black beans
2 cloves garlic
2 tbsp. (30 ml) ginger root
1 tbsp. (15 ml) soy
1 tsp. (5 ml) sugar
1 tbsp. (15 ml) cornstarch
1 tbsp. (15 ml) cold water
1/2-1 c. (125-250 ml) water
garnish with toasted sesame seeds

- Slice lean beef steak thinly into strips and marinate in soy, dry sherry and cornstarch. Even tough cuts of meat become tender when sliced this thinly and marinated.
- Cut onion into wedges, asparagus into two-inch sections, and remaining vegetables into dice, keeping each separate to add to the wok at different times.
- Mush together the dried, fermented black beans, minced garlic and ginger, soy sauce and sugar in a separate bowl to add near the end of cooking.
- Heat a drizzle of oil in a wok and stir fry the onion for a few seconds. Add the mushrooms, then the asparagus, zucchini, and finally the peppers, stir-frying each for a few seconds to a minute before adding the next vegetable.
- Remove to a platter with a slotted spoon.
- Add a drizzle more oil to the wok if needed, heat, then add the beef and marinade and stir fry until most of the pink has gone before adding the black bean mixture.
- Stir-fry with the beef before returning the vegetables to the wok, mixing everything quickly.
- Push it up the sides of the wok, add the cornstarch mixture to the juice in the bottom and stir until it bubbles and thickens. Add more water as needed to make a nice thick sauce.
- Stir-fry everything until the sauce is well mixed in, adding a bit more hot water if needed.
- Garnish with toasted sesame seeds.
- Serves 3-4, more if part of a Chinese meal.

WINE FOR BLACK BEAN BEEF:
I might try a Tinhorn Creek Cabernet Franc with this but just in case the ginger proves unfriendly to the wine, keep some good hoppy ale in reserve.

Ham & Cabbage Chow Mein

Chow mein served in China is quite different from that generally known in North America. This is my version.

1/2 lb. (225 g) egg noodles
1/4 lb. (115 g) ham
2 c. (500 ml) bean sprouts
6 mushrooms
1/2 green cabbage
1 large onion
drizzle of oil
1 tbsp. (15 ml) soy
1/2 c. (125 ml) water
1 tbsp. (15 ml) brown bean sauce
1 tbsp. (15 ml) cornstarch
1 tbsp. (15 ml) cold water

WINE FOR HAM AND CABBAGE CHOW MEIN: *This calls for fruity, exotic whites like Celista's Ortega from the Shuswap or Domaine de Chaberton's Siegerrebe.*

- Cook Chinese egg noodles according to package directions, drain and rinse with cold water and let dry for about an hour before completing the dish.
- Cut ham into matchstick-sized pieces and set aside.
- Rinse bean sprouts and let drain; clean mushrooms and slice.
- Cut cabbage into slices and then strips, and slice onion in half and then into strips, too.
- Heat a large wok or frypan to medium-high and add a drizzle of oil, swirling it around to coat the surface.
- Dump cold, dry noodles in, spread them out and pat them down.
- After they've cooked for a few minutes and begun to crisp up, turn them over to do the other side. When they've browned slightly, turn out onto a warmed serving platter and keep in a low oven.
- Add another drizzle of oil to the wok, add cabbage and stir fry; then onion and mushrooms.
- Stir-fry for a few minutes on medium-high heat. Add ham and stir-fry for a minute.
- Add soy and water, place bean sprouts on top and cover to steam for a few minutes, until the cabbage has greened up and the onions are soft and translucent.
- Don't overcook.
- Remove lid and stir everything together. Push the food aside and add the Chinese brown bean sauce to the liquid in the bottom. Stir well.
- Combine cornstarch and cold water in a tiny bowl.
- When the liquid in the wok returns to bubbling, blend in the cornstarch and cold water mix. As it simmers it will begin to thicken and turn translucent.
- Add hot water as needed, stirring again to create a nice thick sauce. Mix thoroughly with ham and vegetables to glaze everything.
- Pour over noodles and serve.
- Serves 6-8.

Pork or Chicken Fried Rice

Whenever you have a bit of leftover meat such as ham, pork, beef or chicken, it can be turned into a great quick dinner, with a variety of vegetables and some quickly cooked or leftover rice. In fact, cook an extra few pieces of chicken or pork when preparing a meal, then put the extras in the fridge to cut up for fried rice later in the week. I prefer brown rice, but it takes more time, so cook it ahead, or use rice left over from a previous meal. Don't forget to load it up with lots of vegetables.

1 onion
2 stalks celery
3 stalks bok choy
1/2 red pepper
4 mushrooms
4 c. (1 l) cold, cooked rice
1 c. (250 ml) cold, cooked meat
1/4 c. (60 ml) chicken stock
1 tbsp. (15 ml) soy sauce

- Chop vegetables and meat into small dice.
- Heat a drizzle of oil in a large wok and when it's hot, begin adding the vegetables, one at a time, in the order given, stir frying for a minute or two before adding the next.
- Add the cooked rice and break it up, stir frying for a few minutes before clearing the centre of the wok and adding the meat.
- Brown the meat on both sides, then add the chicken stock, soy sauce and stir fry everything. Add more chicken stock or water if it seems too dry, and more soy if it lacks flavour.
- Serve when everything is heated through.
- You could add a cup of peas, broccoli, ribbons of fresh spinach, or any other vegetable that's in the fridge.
- Serves 4.

WINE FOR PORK OR CHICKEN FRIED RICE:
I would recommend a moderately-priced Pinot Noir (there are plenty of good ones) or a Gamay Noir or JoieFarm's PTG Red.

Black Bean Spareribs

There are at least a couple of my family members who demand these for special occasions, so be prepared for your family to love them too. If using side spareribs, I like to simmer them in a big pot of water first, to make them tender and to remove most of the fat. That's not necessary if you buy the more expensive back ribs or baby back ribs, which are leaner and tenderer.

2 lb. (1 kg) spareribs
2 tbsp. (30 ml) fresh ginger
3 cloves garlic
3 tbsp. (45 ml) dried black beans
4 green onions
drizzle of oil
2 tbsp. (30 ml) soy sauce
1 tbsp. (15 ml) sherry
1 tsp. (5 ml) sugar
1/2 c. (125 ml) water
1 tbsp. (15 ml) cornstarch
1 tbsp. (15 ml) cold water

- Separate the ribs by slicing between each.
- Prepare the sauce by mincing the peeled ginger and crushing the garlic cloves.
- Mush together with the Chinese preserved dried black beans. (You could substitute black bean sauce for this mix of ginger, garlic and black beans, but this tastes better.)
- Slice the green onions and set aside.

- Heat a drizzle of oil in a large wok to nearly smoking, then add all the ribs, turning about until they're nicely browned.
- Push them to the side and add the black bean mixture, stirring it about until it's nice and fragrant.
- Add all but a couple of spoonfuls of the green onions, then a mixture of the soy sauce, sherry and sugar. Stir it all together.
- Mix in with the ribs, then pour the water over it all.
- Bring to a boil, then cover and reduce the heat to low, allowing it to simmer for about an hour.
- Turn everything over periodically and make sure there's still a bit of liquid to steam the ribs.
- Combine cornstarch with cold water in a small bowl.
- Remove ribs to a serving platter and keep warm.
- Increase the heat and when the liquid is bubbling, add the cornstarch mixture, stirring until the sauce is thickened and smooth.
- Pour over the ribs and garnish with the remaining green onions.

See photograph on page **207**

WINE FOR BLACK BEAN SPARERIBS: *Ribs call for a robust red like Dunham & Froese's Amicitia Red or Rustico Farm's Last Chance, a blend with some Zinfandel in it.*

Egg Rolls with Pork & Shrimp Filling

I hadn't made egg rolls for years because I won't deep-fry and I hate all the grease associated with it. These, however, I found wonderfully light and yummy, and without the grease. I simply baked them.

3 green onions
1 tbsp. (15 ml) ginger
1 stalk bok choy
4 mushrooms
2 c. (500 ml) bean sprouts
1 tbsp. (15 ml) soy sauce
2 tsp. (10 ml) dry sherry
1/2 tsp. (2 ml) sugar
1/2 tsp. (2 ml) salt
drizzle of oil
1/2 lb. (227 g) lean ground pork
1/4 lb. (113 g) shrimp meat
2 tsp. (10 ml) cornstarch
2 tsp. (10 ml) cold water
12 egg roll wrappers

- Mince green onions and ginger; finely chop bok choy and mushrooms. Rinse bean sprouts and drain.
- Combine soy, sherry, sugar and salt and mix well in a small bowl. Set aside.
- Heat a drizzle of oil in a wok and stir fry the lean pork until just cooked through. Add shelled, minced shrimp or prawns and stir fry until it turns opaque.
- Remove from wok.
- Add another drizzle of oil and stir fry ginger, mushrooms and bok choy. Add green onions and stir fry until vegetables begin to soften. Add bean sprouts and combine, then add soy mixture and stir fry. Return pork and prawn mixture to wok. Combine with vegetables and push everything up the sides of the wok.
- Combine cornstarch and cold water and mix well. Add to centre of the wok and bring to bubbling and stir until thickened.
- Stir everything together and remove from heat.
- Divide mixture into 12.
- Place a spoonful diagonally across the bottom corner of an egg roll wrapper and begin to roll wrapper around it. Fold in sides and continue to roll up. Brush the inside of the triangle at the very end with a little beaten egg or a bit of a flour and water mix, to stick it together and lay that side down on a baking sheet.
- Continue until all 12 are rolled.
- Bake at 375 F for about 25 minutes or until browned.
- Serve at once.

See photograph on page **207**

WINE FOR EGG ROLLS WITH PORK & SHRIMP FILLING: *I prefer to wash down egg rolls with a crisp lager or an apple cider.*

TOP:
Den's Meatloaf & Variations

Recipe on page **182**

BOTTOM:
Spicy Tomato Veggie Pasta

Recipe on page **184**

TOP:
Super Sunny Muffins
Recipe on page 189

BOTTOM:
Tofu & Ginger Vegetables
Recipe on page 198

TOP:
Black Bean Spareribs

Recipe on page **203**

BOTTOM:
Egg Rolls with Pork & Shrimp Filling

Recipe on page **204**

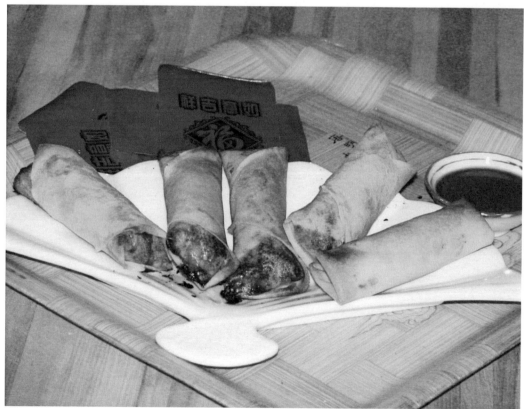

TOP:
Cupcakes with Cream Cheese Filling
Recipe on page **212**

BOTTOM:
Chocolate Sweet Hearts
Recipe on page **214**

ALL FOR LOVE

There's no question about the shape of Valentine's Day: it's a heart.

And, it's a great excuse for indulging your love of decadent foods like rich, dark chocolate.

Make this Valentine's Day fun with a romantic dinner for two or a love-ly dinner for your favourite people. Remember to include the chocolate.

February is not only the month of sleet, snow, icy roads and slushy fields. It's also the month of romance.

The traditions of Valentine's Day may seem silly, but sometimes it helps to forget winter for a moment to focus on chocolate and flowers and those you love.

One of the best expressions of your love, next to flowers of course, is food.

It seems to me that one of the most romantic meals you can have is a fondue for two.

It doesn't matter if it's a nice cheesey one with fresh crusty bread and veggies for dipping and a pile of crisp greens on the side, or a traditional Asian one with bubbling broth in which to cook bits of chicken, prawns, scallops, mushrooms and beef.

There are dozens of lovely dips to serve with such fondues, whether you make your own or pick up some commercially-made ones.

Just by the nature of it, it's a very personal meal, with lots of eye contact and intimacy.

Dim the lights, set a match to the candles, open a bottle of fine B.C. VQA wine and allow some time to linger over your meal...

Cheese fondue is simply wine and cheese melted together with some spices and flavourings, but the variations are endless.

Classically, it's Swiss cheese with dry white wine and kirsch, (which is a cherry brandy), garlic and spices. However, you can make one from cheddar cheese and beer instead, flavouring it with a bit of dry mustard and Worcestershire; or jalapenos, tomatoes and chili sauce.

Be creative and use your imagination. Try whatever sounds like it would taste good.

Accompany it with a glass of bubbly, which is traditional on Valentine's Day, or a fine wine that would pair well with the fondue flavours you've chosen.

For dessert, offer a few chocolate hearts that you've made ahead of time.

If you ever wanted an excuse to show (or remind) someone you love them, Valentine's Day is it.

Cheese Fondue

A fondue is a very romantic way to share a meal. You could consider adding cooked prawns to dip alternately with the bread cubes for a special Valentine's Day treat.

French baguette
1 garlic clove
1/2 lb. (250 g) gruyere cheese
1/2 lb. (250 g) Swiss cheese
2 c. (500 ml) dry white wine
2 tbsp. (30 ml) Kirsch or brandy
2 tbsp. (30 ml) cornstarch
nutmeg, salt and pepper to taste

- Cut bread into bite-sized cubes, with a crust on each so the fondue fork has a firm foundation to hold the tines while it's dunked.
- Squish the garlic clove and rub it enthusiastically around the inside of your fondue pot.
- Cut the cheese into small pieces, or grate it.
- Pour wine into fondue pot and heat until bubbles begin to form before adding a portion of the cheese, perhaps a third, stirring and heating until it melts. Continue, stirring constantly, until all the cheese is in the pot.
- Combine brandy, Kirsch (or apple juice) and cornstarch, re-combining just before mixing it into the bubbling cheese and wine mixture.
- Season with a sprinkle of nutmeg, salt, and white pepper.
- Reduce the heat so the cheese fondue mixture stays hot but doesn't boil or separate, and immediately begin dipping your fresh French bread, stirring the cube on your fork in a figure eight pattern to prevent the mixture from separating.
- Serves 4-8.

WINE FOR CHEESE FONDUE:
The best pairing with cheese fondue that I ever had was in Switzerland, with a bottle of Swiss Chasselas white wine. Here, I would start with the Chasselas from St. Hubertus; but almost any dry white – Pinot Blanc, Pinot Gris, Chardonnay – will deliver a lot of pleasure.

Oriental Fondue

The delicate flavour and texture of seafood is preserved by poaching it in a broth, and boneless chicken simply melts in your mouth. Surprisingly small amounts of different sauces for dipping are all that's required for a leisurely meal. Have a mound of fresh greens to nibble on, alongside.

3 c. (750 ml) broth
1/4 lb. (110 g) beef
1/4 lb. (110 g) chicken
1/4 lb. (110 g) prawns
1/4 lb. (110 g) scallops
mushrooms
peppers
green onions

WINE FOR ORIENTAL FONDUE:
The spicy fruit flavours and aromas of Gewürztraminer will be delicious with this.

DIPPING SAUCES

- Prepare a beef or chicken broth and heat it to boiling on the stove. A home-made chicken stock is preferable, but some commercially-made stocks are also good.
- Slice a tender, lean beef such as rib eye steak into slices, about two inches long and a quarter-inch thick and arrange on a serving plate with similar-sized slices of boneless, skinless chicken breast.
- Shell raw prawns and rinse, and rinse scallops, arranging alongside the chicken and beef.
- Some vegetables could also be cooked in this, but others would need to be partially pre-cooked, then finished off in the bubbling broth.
- Mushrooms, sweet peppers and green onions cook well, but broccoli and cauliflower, potatoes and onions should be partly cooked in advance.
- Consider serving your vegetables alongside, so you can nibble on them while you wait for your meat and seafood to cook.
- Each will take only about a minute to cook through.
- Serves 2.

Cupcakes with Cream Cheese Filling

I remember my Mom removing the centre of cupcakes to stuff them with icing when I was a youngster, so I tried it with a delicious low fat cream cheese icing. It gives the centre surprise a bit more flavour. The result was worth sharing.

CUPCAKES:
These are a low cholesterol version, with no yolks, no butter and just skim milk, but you'd never know it to taste them.

2 c. (500 ml) cake flour
1 1/2 c. (375 ml) sugar
3/4 tsp. (3 ml) salt
1/2 c. (125 ml) oil
1 c. (250 ml) skim milk
1 tbsp. (15 ml) baking powder
4 egg whites
1 tsp. (5 ml) vanilla

■ Pre-heat oven to 350 F.
■ Place paper baking cups in 18 muffin tins.
■ Whisk cake flour in a large mixing bowl with the sugar and salt. Add the oil and half the milk and stir until the flour is mixed in, then beat with a mixer for a minute. Stir in the baking powder, remaining milk, egg whites and vanilla and beat for two minutes.

■ Pour into cupcake papers in muffin tins and bake for 15 to 20 minutes, or until done.
■ Remove and cool before icing.

CREAM CHEESE FILLING:
1 c. (250 ml) light cream cheese
1/2 c. (125 ml) icing sugar
1/2 tsp. (2 ml) vanilla

■ Beat light cream cheese with icing sugar and flavouring until well mixed.
■ Use a paring knife to remove a cone-shaped piece in the centre of each cupcake, stuff the hole with a glob of cream cheese filling and replace the cap.
■ Use a regular butter cream icing to frost the tops and decorate with heart-shaped candy decorations and red sprinkles.

See photograph on page **208**

Sherry & Mixed Peppercorn Dip

This is delicious with beef, chicken and even scallops, as well as veggies that have been cooked in a fondue pot. With other dips this is ample for four or even six people.

4 oz. (125 g) soft cream cheese
1 tbsp. (15 ml) butter
1 tsp. (5 ml) mixed peppercorns
1 garlic clove
1 small gr. onion
1 tsp. (5 ml) dry sherry
sea salt, to taste

- Thoroughly combine soft cream cheese with butter. Coarsely grind a mixture of white, red and black peppercorns, mince garlic and green onion and add with sherry, and sea salt, to taste.
- Mix it all together ahead of time so the flavours blend but don't serve it too cold.

WINE FOR EXCELLENT EASY CHOCOLATE MOUSSE:
I would like a glass of blackberry port with this.

Excellent Easy Chocolate Mousse

This is the easiest, but most delectable dessert ever.

1 1/2 c. (375 ml) light cream
1 lb. (500 ml) chocolate chips
2/3 c. (150 ml) hot coffee
1/2 c. (125 ml) rum
4 eggs
whipped cream
chocolate curls

- Scald light cream and put all ingredients into blender. Blend at high speed two minutes. Pour into little souffle dishes or stemmed dessert glasses and chill. Decorate with whipped cream and chocolate curls or sprinkles before serving. Add a maraschino cherry for color.

Chocolate Sweet Hearts

These are crisp and rich and chocolately, perfect for your favourite valentine, but they are a little bit difficult to work with. Don't try to roll them too thin.

1 c. (250 ml) butter
1 1/2 c. (375 ml) flour
1 c. (250 ml) icing sugar
1/3 c. (75 ml) cocoa

- Pre-heat oven to 300 F.
- Soften the butter, then cream it.
- Whisk flour, sugar and cocoa and gradually mix into butter to form a soft dough.
- Chill the dough, in thirds, if it seems too soft to roll out.
- Roll out a third of the dough on a lightly-floured board to about 1/8-inch in thickness.
- Cut out with a heart-shaped cookie cutter and put on an ungreased cookie sheet. (If decorating with coloured sugar sprinkles or candy hearts, you may wish to do so before baking.)
- Bake for 20 to 25 minutes.
- Cool a bit before removing from the pan.
- These can be decorated with piped frosting or with candy hearts or red and white sugar sprinkles, or a combination of all those.
- Makes about 3 dozen cookies.

See photograph on page **208**

Index of Recipes by Season

Index by Meals

DESSERTS/SWEETS

Cakes/squares

Blueberry Lemon Cake	80
Cupcakes with Cream Cheese Filling	212
Easter Bunny Cake	43
Fudgie Brownies	160
Liz's Chocolate Zucchini Loaf	98
Mom's Apple Coffee Cake	100
Mom's Butterscotchies	190
Mom's Pumpkin Loaf	140
Pat's Apple Chunky	101
Pat's Rhubarb Oat Squares	21

Cookies

Chocolate Sweet Hearts	214
Dad's Cookies	63
Em's Cookies	63
Ginger Snaps	64
Holiday Rum Balls	162
Icebox Spice Cookies	141
Jimmy's Sugar Cookies	159
Pat's Gingerbread	160
Pumpkin Date Cookies	140
Witches' Fingers	133

Desserts

Bernice's Blueberry Buckle	81
Bernice's Chocolate Orange Marble	179
Blueberry Frozen Yogurt	81
Chocolate Easter Egg Nests	42
Cherry Chocolate Cheesecake	79
Cherry Clafoutis	80
Chocolate Raspberry Cheesecake	61
Creamy Berries with Nuts & Chocolate	60
Excellent Easy Chocolate Mousse	213
Fruit Crisp	154
Microwave Rhubarb Crisp	21
Mom's Fruit Surprise	78
Mom's Rum Pudding	166
Pretty Pink Pears	102
Shortcut Shortcakes	59
Watermelon Basket of Fruit	77

Pies

Chocolate-orange Ice Cream Pie	65
Mom's Sour Cream Pie	168
Mom's Maid of Honour Tarts	159
Thelma's Pecan Pie	167

MISCELLANEOUS

Preserves

Grape & Wine Jelly with Jalapenos	105
Pear & Ginger Chutney	103
Mom's Dill Pickles	104

Sauces/salsas

Curry Peanut Sauce	29
Ginger Peach Salsa	90
Lainie's Spicy Salsa	92
Merry Berries	54
Mint Sauce	84
Raspberry Glaze	60

The text type used in this book is PMN Caecilia, a Linotype typeface designed in 1990 by Peter Matthias Noordzij, and named for his wife, Caecilia. He was born in 1961 in The Hague, The Netherlands and is a typographer, type designer and teacher. Because its shapes are humanist rather than geometric, PMN Caecilia is easier on the reader's eye and so more useful as a text typeface than most slab serif designs. The italic particularly has a cursive treatment to some shapes. The result is a face which can be used for text setting as well as display. It is the default typeface on Amazon's Kindle ereader, and is considered one of the more readable typefaces ever designed.

The display type is Runic Condensed, designed at the Monotype Type Drawing Office in 1935, about which was written, "A work of art does not have to be beautiful, but it will need to be displayed with some discretion if it is to have the desired impact. Runic Condensed should be seen as belonging to this category. Used with care nevertheless, it has considerable merit where attention is being courted."

Creative
Engagement

THE OKANAGAN INSTITUTE IS A GROUP OF CREATIVE PROFESSIONALS THAT HAVE GATHERED AROUND THE GOAL OF PROVIDING EVENTS, PUBLICATIONS AND SERVICES OF INTEREST TO ENQUIRING MINDS IN THE OKANAGAN. WE PARTNER WITH INDIVIDUALS, ORGANIZATIONS, INSTITUTIONS AND BUSINESSES TO ACHIEVE OPTIMAL CREATIVE AND SOCIAL IMPACT. OUR MISSION IS TO IGNITE CULTURAL TRANSFORMATION, CATALYZE COLLABORATIVE ACTION, BUILD NETWORKS AND FOSTER SUSTAINABLE CREATIVE ENTERPRISES. WE PROVIDE INNOVATIVE CONSULTATION, FACILITATION, PROFESSIONAL DEVELOPMENT AND CREATIVE SERVICES.

WWW.OKANAGANINSTITUTE.COM